FINGERS CROSSED NO MATTER THE TOSS

HEAL WITH ME THROUGH CANCER

Priyanka Niraj Agarkar

BLUEROSE PUBLISHERS
India | U.K.

Copyright © Priyanka Niraj Agarkar 2025

All rights reserved by author. No part of this publication may be reproduced, stored in a retrieval system or transmitted in any form or by any means, electronic, mechanical, photocopying, recording or otherwise, without the prior permission of the author. Although every precaution has been taken to verify the accuracy of the information contained herein, the publisher assumes no responsibility for any errors or omissions. No liability is assumed for damages that may result from the use of information contained within.

BlueRose Publishers takes no responsibility for any damages, losses, or liabilities that may arise from the use or misuse of the information, products, or services provided in this publication.

For permissions requests or inquiries regarding this publication, please contact:

BLUEROSE PUBLISHERS
www.BlueRoseONE.com
info@bluerosepublishers.com
+91 8882 898 898
+4407342408967

ISBN: 978-93-7018-695-8

Cover Design: Aman Sharma
Typesetting: Pooja Sharma

First Edition: March 2025

This book is dedicated to my mom and dad.

"My mom is my strength and my dad, my courage. Thank you for everything ♥"

Me Tumchya sobat ajun rahanar
Tumhi himmat haru naka.

Tumhi majhi himmat aahat pappa

"I will stay with you longer. Don't lose courage.
You are my strength, Dad."

Detailed Synopsis

This is the story of 23-year-old , a young lady navigating the difficulties of a typical life. As she grew older, struggled with insecurities and frequently felt the pressure of social norms. In her early school years, she faced body image issues due to being a bit heavy, and later, the pressure of competition and constant comparison led her to criticize herself.

She moved to a different city for her studies, made a separate world for herself and became entangled in the never- ending rat race. In her twenties, she found herself unemployed, financially dependent on her parents, and still pursuing a degree with an uncertain future. Amidst these difficulties, health problems surfaced, which many doctors first wrote off as a typical viral cough. But then her life took a sudden turn that pulled her out of the rat race and left her family shaken.

She was diagnosed with a rare type of lung cancer that accounts for less than 1% of all cases, and it was already in stage 4. For a long time, her father kept the severity of her condition hidden. Her mother, father, sister, close friends, and mentor stood by her side throughout the journey, becoming her pillars of strength. She was determined and motivated as she dealt with the difficulties of her treatment. She experienced hair loss, weight gain, and other difficult side effects after the first chemotherapy itself. Despite finishing these six chemotherapy cycles, she discovered that her battle was far from over, as doctors prescribed another twelve maintenance chemotherapy cycles. She was exhausted, had never experienced the fear of death, and had been thrust into life's most significant battle - the fight for her own life.

In her case, doctors couldn't predict when her chemotherapy would end because there was no alternative medicine and other options were unavailable. Throughout her journey, she learned many profound and often painful lessons about her health, frustration, relationships, and helplessness.

In the face of life's uncertainty, she started looking into how to find happiness and progress towards her goals without focusing too much on cancer, while also prioritizing her health more than anything else. She recognized that mental and physical health are inextricably linked and that while doctors can help with physical health, managing one's mind is a personal journey.

She began fathoming the following:

1. Everything else is super important until you realize that the only thing that matters is your health, which includes mental health as well.

2. Achieving self-acceptance takes practice.

3. You are enough for yourself to fathom and cover all the wounds in your heart.

4. One day at a time! Nothing is going to last forever.

5. It's all in our heads. Competition and comparison are good until they're healthy. The moment it starts stressing you out, you should know where to stop and snap out of it, and it can be done when you understand this one simple thing: time is a real thing, everybody has their unique timeline, and you need to have immense faith in yourself that you will do something good with your life.

6. The mind has immense healing powers. The brain questions whether miracles could ever happen, whereas the mind believes and makes them happen!

7. How to face the fear of death.

8. Never wrestle with your emotions. Release yourself from the pressure of being all sunshine and rainbows when all you feel inside is like the lead character in a melodrama. It's important to vent it out.

9. Sometimes you have to have the courage to let go of things and people you love for yourself; you have to choose yourself, and it is difficult to believe that there will be better days in life when you feel complete and content. Till then, it's practice. Practice imagining that completeness within you. Learn again to imagine like a kid and allow yourself to feel happy in the moment where you'd always wanted to see yourself. Push yourself a little bit more each day with your imagination.

10. There's a lot to learn from books, mistakes, and people, irrespective of their age.

11. If you want to achieve the ultimate goal of life, which is happiness, you need not think of the future; you have to go back to being a child.

12. Hold onto hope. Hope is what will get you through.

13. You are more than what you think about yourself.

14. Keep your loved ones close. With genuine people, you'll notice that nothing is forced.

15. Just a smidge of Confidence can get you a long way.

The book will end in a way as if Akira were writing a journal, starting with,

"Dear diary,

This is my journey so far. I am still in the midst of my treatment, on maintenance chemotherapy to prevent recurrence in the future, and it is a long way after the treatment as well, but I have learned so much up to this point and will continue to do so. One of the most important things cancer has taught me is that you don't have to be a certain way to enjoy your life and be happy and content. Happiness and peace should not be conditional. Today, I am happy and content with whatever I am, and I accept it. I have my fingers crossed in the hope that years later, when I reread this journal, I'll be proud of myself for not giving up, no matter what toss."

Acknowledgments

This book is a reflection of my journey, one that would not have been possible without the support and belief of the people around me.

I am deeply grateful to my parents, whose endless love, encouragement, and confidence in me have been my pillars of strength. Their unwavering support has shaped me into the person I am today. Thanks to my mother, whose nurturing presence has been my constant source of love and support. She has always been there to lift me up, provide comfort in my hardest moments, and offer her wisdom when I needed it most. Her boundless faith in me and her dedication to our family have inspired me to keep going, even when the path seemed unclear. She is, and will always be, the heart of this journey.

A heartfelt thanks to my sister and my mentor, Mr. B.M. Chaturvedi, for their invaluable contributions to this book. Their ideas, guidance, and effort in helping me bring this story to life have been nothing short of extraordinary. Your time, effort, and wisdom have been instrumental in shaping my work and my approach to writing. You have helped me navigate this creative journey with clarity, and your influence will always be a part of this book.

I am also thankful to my friends—Aditi, Komal, Umang, and Vaidehi—who have been a constant source of encouragement and positivity throughout this journey. Each of you has played a unique role in helping me stay motivated, providing thoughtful suggestions, and offering words of comfort when I needed them most. Your unwavering belief in me and your collective energy gave me the strength to push forward, even during the toughest moments.

To each of you, thank you for being an essential part of my journey and for making this book a reality.

Author Bio

Priyanka Niraj Agarkar is a vibrant 23-year-old from Akola, Maharashtra. In her cozy world, she is surrounded by her parents' loving embrace and a loved sister. Priyanka began her academic career at Pune University, where she earned her stripes in BCom, laying the groundwork for her future endeavors.

Priyanka is currently immersed in the dynamic realm of the Company Secretary course's Final Level, navigating the intricate corridors of corporate expertise.

Beyond the formalities of her education, however, she is a passionate soul with a symphony in her heart. Her musical partners are the keyboard and guitar, and her affection extends to every musical instrument that graces her world.

Priyanka finds solace and self-expression through rhythmic chords and harmonious melodies.

However, life has a way of orchestrating unexpected melodies. When she was diagnosed with cancer, this young woman faced a formidable challenge. Faced with adversity, she resolved to cultivate new habits, and one such endeavor led her to the captivating world of literature. Priyanka, who was not a natural

reader, discovered the magic of books during her illness. She was captivated by the wonder of how diverse minds could weave stories and thoughts together. It was a revelation that piqued her interest in not only consuming but also

contributing to this rich tapestry of narratives. Priyanka's journey as a writer

began with this realization. Writing became her haven, a place where she could express herself and channel her emotions. With no prior writing experience,

Priyanka embraced the blank page, understanding that every writer has to

begin from scratch. Her words are a testament to perseverance and a reminder that creativity has the power to overcome obstacles.

Today, Priyanka aspires to be not only a reader and writer but a storyteller whose words resonate with others. Despite adversity, her journey is one of

courage, passion, and the transformative power of literature. Priyanka Agarkar continues to compose her symphony of life with every word she writes on paper.

About the Co-Author

The co-author of this book, Niraj Agarkar, is not only Priyanka's father but also her unwavering source of strength and encouragement. A seasoned tax consultant, Niraj has spent his career mastering the complexities of taxation and financial planning. Beyond his professional expertise, he is known for his lively personality and ability to bring positivity to every situation.

As a co-author, Niraj has played a pivotal role in shaping this book. His insightful contributions, coupled with his steadfast support for Priyanka's vision, ensured this story was brought to life with depth and heart. Niraj's involvement reflects not just his pride in Priyanka's resilience but also his shared belief in the transformative power of storytelling.

Together, this father-daughter duo has crafted a narrative that celebrates hope, strength, and the profound connections that sustain us through life's challenges.

Contents

Chapter 1: Introduction 1

Chapter 2: Heaven is nothing but home................................ 4

Chapter 3 9

Chapter 4: When your own is in pain, how to be their aid?.. 16

Chapter 5: Happy new year!.. 24

Chapter 6 28

Chapter 7 33

Chapter 8 42

Chapter 9: Fear of death... 49

Chapter 10 56

Chapter 11: Hope is fragile 66

Chapter 12 71

Chapter 13 76

Chapter 14: How one mentor in your life can be catalyst of change 84

Chapter 15: Ultimate goal 89

Chapter 16 95

Chapter 17: Elephant in the room 104

Chapter 18 108

Chapter 19 115

Chapter 20: Living beyond the limits................................. 123

Chapter 1
Introduction

When life knocks you down and drags you to rock bottom, ensure your ears are hooked to your rock playlist. Oh, and crank up the volume. – Dad's Precept Diary

When I was a kid, my father often pushed me to write precepts, brief nuggets of wisdom that he believed could illuminate life's path.

With contagious zeal, he'd declare, "With time it will all make sense. When I am not around, you shall have my precepts diary and I will guide you through it. Even if I am around, it will help you because this diary has all my learnings and you should have your own. All the tumbles and fumbles and how you found your way through it, growing and humble." I often wondered how just a few lines could help me during life's most trying times. Today, four years later, I opened his precept diary, hoping to find answers to the questions gnawing at my curiosity.

So far, it's evident that life plays by its own rules; it doesn't always adhere to the plans you meticulously craft in your life's blueprint. The universe, in its enigmatic way, unfolds a narrative you never could have anticipated. As I went about my daily errands, lost in my world, I had set unreasonable expectations for myself and the world around me. I had been so relentlessly hard on myself, so unreasonably critical, that I had lost sight of something essential—appreciating not only myself but also every precious gift life had bestowed upon me. I failed to recognize the value of my existence and the richness of the world around me until it was all cruelly snatched away.

After pouring my heart and thoughts into the journal's pages, I pushed myself up from the chair, feeling the weight of exhaustion in my heavy head and weary eyes. My body practically begged for a pick-me-up in the form of a nice, hot cup of tea, something minty and ginger-spiced to revive my spirits. So, I dashed downstairs to the kitchen, whipping up that cup of tea just the way my body craved it – minty with a ginger kick. Out on the balcony, I sipped it slowly, soaking in the nature show that unfolded, painting a serene picture that was nothing short of eye candy.

The sky donned its beautiful colors, making a captivating cameo that you just couldn't afford to miss. I was completely mesmerized and lost in my thoughts and had a flashback. Not long ago, I stood on the balcony, holding that same cup of tea, savoring it with the enthusiasm of a kid with candy. But the person in that memory? Well, she was a whole different character; I'd say, she was much more confused and living her life on the surface, even though she seemed like she was in a rush to get somewhere, caught in a never-ending race.

It's as if the universe decided to play a game with her, to change her for good, can say. The story of this girl is probably the story of many of you. The things she cried over, her mistakes, her lessons, and her experiences might resonate with you. In a world filled with insincere sympathy, we all yearn to be truly understood by someone. This girl, or my old self to be precise, now only exists in the pages of my journal. She's trapped there, crying, seeking empathy, searching for her whys, thinking she's not worthy enough or is not enough to fathom and heal all the wounds of her heart. It took some time for her to realize that all this while, she held the answers to her prayers, or if I may, she was the solution to her riddles.

Let's open that journal and step back to a time when I was standing in the same place on the balcony. Let's start from the get-go and see where she takes herself and you.

(Cracking open that time capsule of a journal) And my phone started buzzing.

Chapter 2
Heaven is nothing but home

There it was— a call from Ishika. Our profile picture showed us in full-on laughter mode, probably over some absurdly silly thing.

I picked up, already knowing what she was going to say, "Hey, when you're back at the hostel, you've got to hook me up with a killer haircut." She said it like she meant business. "And let's not mess around with our lectures; those exams are just three months away."

I mumbled my agreement, my mind ping-ponging between our conversation and reverie.

If I were to describe a person, Ishika, in brief, she's the epitome of the generosity of spirit. People like her are an extraordinary rarity. You have unlimited access to full support and entertainment for the rest of your life. The foundation of our bond is so strong, like a rock in the middle of a storm. We first met in our freshman year of college, and ever since then, we've been joined at the hip. She is my soulmate and a roommate too. YES! You can find your soulmate in friendships as well.

I guess the reason that we just hit it off instantly is that we live by the same principles. We have the same brain wave when it comes to morals and values and we both are hilarious, at least to us and we couldn't care less about what others think. Above all, I know I can count on her wholeheartedly.

The very next moment, I was already in packing mode, tossing essentials into my bag, all set for a quick return to the hostel. There's always this strange feeling that creeps in when I'm about to leave home for my studies. It's amazing how you can deeply adore and miss something, yet simultaneously have this itch to go away for your good. And when you come back, that sense of belonging feels profoundly pure and totally your own. You just know that, no matter what, you can always come back and take shelter beneath its warmth. Now, for you, that could be anyone or anything. For me, it's my family, my home – mom, dad, and my young one who by the way decided to look like the elder one because yeah, she's taller than me.

She'd always tease me about that saying, "Funny how even at twenty-three you have a baby face that looks like 10 years old, it's hard for anyone to take you seriously with that face." And she'd give herself a good laugh. Younger- siblings are living proof that you can unconditionally love someone yet wish to beat them up badly after a wild chase. I was nearly done packing my bags when, out of nowhere, a knock echoed through the door. Speak of the devil and here she is, my sister, Bhumi, showing up like she read my mind!

She stormed into my room, clutching packets of chips and a chilled can of cold coffee, instantly making herself at home. She was wearing my blue tee she'd sneakily swiped from my closet when I was out, something I'd never have allowed otherwise.

And started yapping about how on the way to the grocery shopping with Mom, who had initially planned to buy just a few things but somehow ended up with twenty extra items in the cart. She was fuming about it and even vented her frustration at Bhumi on the way home for being impatient. But I don't blame Bhumi, my mom can be difficult sometimes only while shopping, otherwise she's the nicest person and too good for this world.

"You're leaving today, right?" Bhumi inquired. "Just make sure you're not taking any of my clothes with you. You always sneak them away, and I end up searching for my stuff. And one day, I'll stumble upon your post on Instagram, and there'll be my jeans," she warned, her eyes narrowing with suspicion.

I smiled a little because she was right and I was planning to take one of her tees with me, but I am going to take it anyway. I love to piss her off.

she grumbled loudly.

"Also, there's this girl in my college who's incredibly annoying. Honestly, the whole college gets on my nerves, and I can't stand it. She started going on about how she and her boyfriend fight over trivial things and how cute it is. If I were in her place, I'd lose it over that so-called 'cuteness'. I had to take some deep, calming breaths to prevent myself from screaming right in her face. Stupid people."

I listen to her rant as I finish packing and close the zip of my bag. A random thought comes to my mind - *I need to plan a trip with my roommates to someplace nice.* My sister is still yapping about her college and how she can't stand it, but my thoughts were consumed by how to convince my roommates to go on a trip. Of course, they'd be interested, but getting them to agree on anything was always a bit of a challenge. We had exams looming just three months away, so planning it now seemed somewhat pointless. However, I was determined to make it happen. After all, we wouldn't all be in the same city forever. In a year or two, who knew where we'd end up – different cities, maybe even different countries for work. I knew I had to make this year count. With that in mind, I dragged my bags downstairs, knowing I had to head to my hostel in the next three hours.

"What will you have for supper?" Mom asked.

"I'll have something light, a sandwich or rice maybe?" I replied confusingly.

"Make sure you take care of yourself over there, eat well, get some exercise, and most importantly, stop using earphones while driving, and..." Mom began, giving me her list of guidelines.

I interrupted her, rolling my eyes and saying, "I know Mom! Don't worry, I will be good, I promise."

I really should do something about my habit of cranking up the volume on my earphones while driving. I've noticed a slight ache in my left ear, probably because of that, but I haven't mentioned it to anyone. It's not too bad, so I've just been ignoring it.

Dad on his way back home, brought back a load of snacks for me. I packed them in my bag and hugged everyone as I prepared to head out. My mom had tears in her eyes, and she always gets emotional when I leave home for my Studies.

But this time, something felt off. As I left, I was filled with a lot of anxiety. I tried to convince myself that it was probably because I hadn't left home for a long time, which was making me feel this way.

However, looking back, I realize it was a sign.

Dad came to drop me off at the station. The hostel is ten hours away from home and I prefer the night journey most of the time. I kept my luggage under the seat and went to the gate as the train started to leave to say goodbye. I came back inside, assembled my blanket and everything on the birth, and went to sleep with a happy and excited feeling in my heart.

I woke up the next morning with the warmth of the sunshine coming from the train's window. On the way from the station to the hostel is my favourite road, covered with bushes and trees, listening to my playlist. There was a lot of calmness in my head and heart, nature has that power.

Chapter 3

If time morphs in its cryptic way, be a Chameleon

I reached the hostel in the morning and called Ishika for help with getting my luggage upstairs. The moment she spotted me, she rushed over and enveloped me in a tight hug.

"Thank goodness you're back! I was getting so hungry that I even called Vaya to find out when she'd be back at the hostel so we could have breakfast together," Ishika exclaimed.

"It feels so good to be back. It's been so long since the three of us were together. I can't even recall the last time we hung out. I wonder what Vaya has been up to all this time," I mused.

"I did not hear much from Vaya. We were definitely in touch but only on WhatsApp. I miss her." Said Ishika.

"Yeah same, me too." I agreed.

Vaya and I are like partners in crime. We share similar interests when it comes to having fun and have a knack for bringing out each other's obscene sides. I first met Vaya in extra classes but after a year we became roommates. Our favorite pastime was exploring new food joints, all ready to eat our weight in food. I can still vividly recall the day I first met Vaya. The classroom was crowded with a hundred unfamiliar faces, and the rooms seemed vast. It was my first time away from home, and uncertainty would strike at random moments, filling me with anxiety. I found myself perched on the front row, battling my nervousness when I noticed a hand enthusiastically waving at me, accompanied by a broad, welcoming smile. It was Vaya, inviting me to sit beside her, and it instantly eased my worries. She has been my savior since then. Classes would've been an impossible task without her.

Ishika, Vaya, and I - our trio felt like a second home to us. We were inseparable, looking out for each other, studying together, and occasionally getting on each other's nerves.

"Hey!" came a voice from behind as we made our way up the stairs. It was Vaya, the missing third piece of our beautiful puzzle. Curly hair, brown eyes, and a smile on her face. If I were to metaphorically describe us, both Ishika and Vaya would be like golden retrievers, all sunshine and sunflowers, true extroverts who excel in expressing themselves. Meanwhile, I'd be more like a chunky cat or a cactus – cute but ouch, usually introverted and selectively extroverted.

As we kept the luggage in our room, the next moment we were sitting in an aesthetic café, having our go-to breakfast: Bun-Maska paired with a steaming cup of tea. The café had a charming ambiance, and every bite and sip felt just right. And it strikes me that this is the right time to talk about the thought that was lingering around my head for so long.

"Here's what I think. Once we are done with our exams, let's take a trip together", I said excitedly.

"Great idea, let's just go in a group. You can ask your cousins too", Vaya said to Ishika.

"Yes, and you can ask Jim if he'd be interested", said Ishika.

"Yes! I'll convince him but I don't think he's going to turn it down", I said while pressing my left ear as it was slightly aching again.

It's been a few months since I started dating Jim. I've been lucky to have found a guy like him in a world full of hookup culture and casual dating. Our generation's dating culture is trash, he's just a golden trash. This line sums up our bond perfectly. We can roast each other, test each other's patience, and then simply head out for a great meal, leaving any grudges behind. And I think that's how it should be.

I texted Jim, throwing out a casual invite, "Up for a trip? We haven't settled on a destination yet, but there should be about 7-8 of us. Should be a blast."

Jim read the message and got back to me in about 2 minutes, with a simple "Count me in."

I shared Jim's confirmation with Ishika and Vaya and a few more thumbs-ups came in.

After our wholesome and filling breakfast, we strolled out of the café. I reached into my pocket, pulled out my earphone case, and popped one earphone into my right ear, enjoying my ride back to the hostel.

I was feeling tired somehow, maybe because of the traveling, and I wasn't regular with my workout as well. I knew I needed to hit the gym today to kick away the lethargy that was hitting me. I have been health-conscious for as long as I can remember. I always worried about the shape that I was in. Constantly beat myself up, if I'd gain a few extra kgs. From dealing with childhood bullies to navigating the lingering insecurities as I grew up, I became the highest critic of myself.

"Why can't we just stay kids forever?" I pondered quietly, reminiscing about some cherished moments from my childhood. During those years, we lived within our bubble, blissfully oblivious to the complexities of the universe.

However, the bubble burst with the blaring horns of passing cars as we made our way back to the hostel. Suddenly, I became acutely aware of my surroundings and the ache in my ear.

As I reached the hostel, it instantly gave me the feeling of home. The small, snug room was cramped for three people and their clothes, but it held a certain tranquility. Despite its snugness, the room featured three windows that offered views of lush greenery and allowed the cheerful melodies of chirping birds to filter in. We had this peculiar thing where we'd chat with the bird outside our window by mimicking its chirps, convinced that it could understand us and would respond with even more enthusiastic chirping.

Vaya and I began unpacking our bags and organizing our respective sections. As I delved into the task, I stumbled upon a baby picture of myself. In that snapshot, I was a mere two or three years old, cradled in my dad's arms, sporting a grin so wide it looked as if someone had wedged a coat hanger in my mouth.

Since as far back as my memory stretches, growing up amidst the ever-changing landscape of life, I've absorbed a fundamental truth down to my very core: the importance of self-reliance. Not just the financial kind, mind you, but the emotional kind as well. This philosophy instilled in me an insatiable drive, not for the applause of the world, but to prove it to the most demanding critic of all – myself. It's like having a perpetual zest for self-affirmation, a rush to validate my capabilities, a quest for personal triumph, all wrapped up in a neat little package of independence.

Seeing that innocent, carefree smile made me ponder – where did that carefree baby disappear to? When did I start caring so much about the world and its opinions that I forgot to care about myself? When did I sign up for this relentless race to secure a job in my twenties, maintain a perfect physique, and accumulate higher degrees, all within society's designated timeline?

I was unhappy because I had been trying too hard to fit into these norms. In my twenties, I found myself jobless, financially reliant on my parents, and still pursuing a degree whose ultimate destination in life remained uncertain.

Amidst the chaotic jumble of thoughts in my head, I decided to tackle the mess of clothes and stuff cluttering my cupboard. Gym time was looming, and even though I wasn't particularly feeling up to it, I mustered the willpower to show up. After some warm-up and core exercises, a nagging strain crept into my upper left back, swiftly followed by a sharp pain. I turned to my coach, pleading for stretches to alleviate the discomfort, but to no avail. The pain persisted, so I made my way to a local doctor, who swiftly diagnosed it as a mild strain from an exercise gone wrong.

A few painkillers managed to dull the ache, and although I still felt a bit worn out, I convinced myself it was just because I hadn't worked out in a while. So, I resolved to continue with my daily half-hour workouts.

Post-gym escapade, I gave Kyra a ring to fill her in on my gym mishap. She suggested some stretching exercises, and our conversation meandered into random territories. I've known Kyra since the school days, and I can still vividly recall our first encounter. It was the seventh grade, and we were both new to the school. I'd been through some tough times with a teacher in my previous school during sixth grade, so my parents decided it was time for a change. On that fateful first day, I walked into the classroom to find Kyra sitting at the teacher's desk, sizing up everyone who entered like a hawk. Like any good story, we've had our fair share of ups and downs over the past 10 years. From supporting each other through the most naïve decisions to weathering the consequences of our actions and learning from our mistakes, we've been through it all.

Thinking back on those school days brings a weird mix of happiness and nostalgia. Waking up in the morning, neatly plaiting our hair and donning our uniforms, scribbling notes behind our textbooks during lectures, belting out a loud and boisterous "good morning Ma'aaaaam", sneakily pulling someone's chair from under them and then collapsing in giggles, only to face the wrath of the teacher, or occasionally being sent out of the classroom. Annual days, sports days, carnival days, celebrating every little occasion, and then suddenly realizing as school ended that those days would never return. I can still recall, and it's rather funny, how Kyra and I used to sneak into the bathroom to shed a few tears over the impending end of our school days, only to put on cool faces once we returned to class. Adi and I became tighter than ever post-school, but the escapades we had back in our school days – those memories are something else, you know? They're like a treasure trove of good vibes and nostalgia that can't be recreated. It's the kind of stuff that makes you feel all warm and fuzzy inside, like a cozy hug from your past. Whenever I needed practical advice or a dose of brutal honesty, Adi was the go-to person. Having people who would hold up a mirror to show you the unvarnished truth, no matter how brutal, is essential.

But life takes a dramatic turn after school, and we evolve as individuals. We've witnessed each other's growth. There were times when we couldn't be there for each other during the worst of times due to work or studies, given our different fields, but we always managed to find a way to connect, even if it was just for half an hour or ten minutes. We've truly been through it all.

As Kyra and I chatted away, I didn't even realize that a couple of hours had slipped by. The pain in my back still lingered, despite the medications. I chose to ignore it. The exams were coming closer, so I was much more focused on my preparations. I went to the library after having a cup of coffee. Ishika and Vaya were already there. So, I joined them.

Later I got a text from Jim. I had a date with him the next day. I was going to see him after so many days.

"I have a surprise for you", read his last message.

Chapter 4
When your own is in pain, how to be their aid?

The next morning, I joined Jim for breakfast at our beloved South Indian eatery, where we indulged in some mouthwatering Podi Idli. For the uninitiated, 'Podi' is this delectable spice blend that they serve with a generous drizzle of ghee, alongside idli, and accompanied by chutney and sambar on the side. It's been our breakfast ritual ever since. Of course, after breakfast, we couldn't resist the allure of a hot cup of tea. So, we grabbed some takeaway tea and strolled down the street. This particular road was like a painting – picturesque and exuding tranquility. We walked a fair distance, and as fatigue set in, I couldn't hold back my curiosity any longer. I prodded Jim about the surprise. And, that's when he whipped out two tickets to a music concert, featuring his all-time favorite band, set to hit the city in just a month's time. I was very excited, as it would be my first ever experience of attending a live music concert.

But before attending that, I'd a month's time to cover the major chunk of my studies for exams so I could enjoy the concert guilt-free.

There were a lot of things happening this month. We needed to plan for Ishika's birthday, but there was a small hiccup – she had fallen sick with a viral cough. I hoped she'd get better before her big day. Actually, for the trip we had in mind, Vaya and I decided to surprise her by setting up a beautiful hillside decor, providing a panoramic view of the entire city along with a stunning sunset to make it a picture-perfect moment. To get things rolling, we had to fetch a bunch of stuff today.

By the afternoon, I was already feeling a bit worn out, and the nagging upper back pain kept poking at me. But you know how it is; we often choose to ignore those warning signs. So, Vaya and I went to the local general store mall to buy everything we needed for the birthday decoration, and we even convinced her cousin to pitch in. By the time we got back to the hostel, having survived the day, we were utterly drained. You know, there are days when you work so hard that it feels like sleep's gone on a vacation, and doesn't come to visit at night. I was battling fatigue, and the painkillers I'd taken earlier were my best friends at that point. The doctor had assured me that the pain would ease as I finished the medication course, and she was right. The next morning, I woke up feeling considerably better.

So, in the morning, Vaya, Ishika, and I decided to head to our favorite spot near the hostel. There's this scenic hill where we often go to catch some fresh air, and the view from there is simply breathtaking. Today was extra special because, while we were there, we met an uncle who had three adorable dogs. These furry pals were so endearing that we couldn't resist playing with them, and taking loads of pictures. The surprising part was that these three doggos were incredibly well-trained, posing for every photo as if they were seasoned supermodels. It reminded me of Milo. Milo's the reason I grew to love dogs; otherwise, I used to be quite wary of them. I can still vividly recall the very first-time Ishika introduced me to Milo, the furry resident of her sister's house. Whenever we found ourselves in the clutches of homesickness, we knew where to find solace – her sister's place and Milo was the ultimate remedy. So, on one fine day, the three of us embarked on a visit for a hearty meal. Now, let me set the stage for you. It appeared that Milo had been taken out for a leisurely stroll prior to our arrival. As we gathered around the dining table, eagerly digging into our meal, our unsuspecting companion returned from his walk. At this point, I must emphasize that Milo was no ordinary dog. Hyperactive would be an understatement. And during those days, I happened to be particularly apprehensive about our four-legged friends. You know the type of dogs

I'm talking about, right? Those enthusiastic furballs that can't wait to shower you with their love, often charging at you, barking with unwavering zeal, and demanding copious amounts of attention. Well, Milo was the poster pup for this breed of boundless enthusiasm. Milo sprinted toward me, barking like there was no tomorrow. I, mistakenly thinking that Milo was furious with me, made a run for it, still clutching my meal. I dashed off in fear, and Milo chased me, barking all the way. Ishika and Vaya joined in the chase. Eventually, it became clear that all Milo wanted was to sniff me and say hello. So, I stopped running, and we hit it off. From that day forward, I was no longer scared of dogs. It was a hilarious first meeting between me and Milo, a memory that still makes us laugh when we talk about it.

As we descended from the hill, we sat down for breakfast, basking in the tranquil atmosphere. I have this habit of returning to nature every now and then. We have a beautiful connection with nature. Nature is content with its own being, neither desiring too much nor too little. It encompasses both light and darkness. There's no right or wrong in nature; things simply exist and evolve with time. We're no different; we just need to learn to give things some time.

After breakfast, we headed to the library. We were planning to leave tomorrow for our two-day trip. Vaya, Ishika's cousin, and I set out early because we had to go to the birthday decoration spot first to prepare for Ishika's surprise. But before we even set off, I also caught a viral cough. Just when the upper back pain was easing, the cough kicked in. The location we had chosen for the birthday surprise was so stunning that on one side, you'd see all the hills, and on the other, the city lights. As the sun set behind the hills, you'd get a breathtaking view, and along with it, the city lights would begin to twinkle. It was quite chilly there, and my cough worsened.

I knew I'd need to see a local doctor once I got back from our trip. Despite that, we had a fantastic time during our journey. Ishika's birthday surprise unfolded exactly as we had planned. As soon as we returned, I booked an appointment with a doctor who diagnosed me with a viral cough. I completed the prescribed course of medicines, although it didn't provide much relief for my cough.

On the way back to my hostel, I received a call from Bhumi, informing me that I might need to be at home with her. My parents were about to embark on a trip to Bali with their friends, and since Bhumi would be home alone, she needed me to be there. I considered getting checked by our family doctor since I was going home.

Dad arranged the train ticket reservation for me as I would be leaving for home in two days. I was going to spend a week at home because my mother had her monthly checkup scheduled. My parents decided to have her checkup done immediately upon their return from the trip. I, on the other hand, was quite anxious because her routine checkup was related to her past battle with cancer.

Three years ago, my mother was diagnosed with breast cancer, and it was the toughest and most bewildering period in my life. Many things have stabilized in my mind with time, but when you have to go through situations where there's a fear that you might lose a loved one, that fear, disbelief, confusion, and the feeling of helplessness are truly indescribable. You're left not knowing what to do or say.

To cope with my anxiety, I reached out to Adi because she had been through a similar situation. Her mother is also a cancer survivor, and I had seen Adi go through that challenging period back in school. She never really spoke about anything related to that matter, but I believed that she would understand what I was going through better than anyone else. As we conversed, I realized that the situation was strikingly similar to one where we were initially kept in the dark, only to discover it later. I came to know about it when I saw my mother's hair falling out, and then I stumbled upon one of the reports, which

revealed to me, to a significant extent, it's cancer. The same thing happened with Adi. I distinctly remember how hard it was to believe, and I couldn't find the words to express my thoughts. All that raced through my mind was a simple question: why?

Since then, I used to be a bit anxious about my mom's regular checkups. However, she has made an incredible recovery in the past two years, so I wasn't that worried this time. As I was conversing with Adi, I noticed that my cough had worsened. I found myself coughing every five minutes, and Ishika was going through the same ordeal. Therefore, before leaving for home, I borrowed some cough medicine from her.

Vaya came to drop me off at the station, and on our way, we stopped at a café for a coffee break. I ordered a delightful blend of hazelnut and coffee with a scoop of vanilla ice cream. It tasted heavenly, but my stomach didn't agree. As I headed back home, I kept throwing up due to my rebellious stomach, and by the time I reached home in the morning, I was feeling sick.

My mom promptly took me to our family doctor, who confirmed that he had been seeing a lot of patients lately with cough complaints. The fatigue I was experiencing was attributed to the cough. While I was at home, my mom generously dispensed various home remedies for cough relief. They did help alleviate the pain I felt in my throat from coughing so forcefully.

The pain in my upper left back also reared its head, and this time, it was so severe that I had to resort to painkiller injections.

According to the doctor, I had a calcium deficiency, which was prolonging the healing process of the muscle I had injured during my workout. It eventually healed after completing the course of medications, or so I thought.

The cough was proving to be a persistent nuisance. It would temporarily subside during medication but return once the course was completed. So, I sought a second opinion from another doctor, who diagnosed it as a viral cough. I was told not to worry too much about it, as it was a common issue due to the changing weather, affecting nearly every third person. The remedy was to complete the prescribed medicine doses, and the cough would eventually subside. However, the medication suppressed the cough only temporarily, and during a follow-up, the doctor added an inhaler to my treatment. Upon returning home from the hospital, I felt utterly drained, and the fatigue had firmly taken hold. However, my weariness was soon replaced by a call from Dad, who delivered the heartening news that my mom's reports were all clear, and they would be returning home the next day. It was a relief to hear.

Throughout the week, Bhumi and I had a great time. If we put my pesky cough aside, everything else was pure fun. We ventured out, explored new food joints, engaged in good-natured spats over the last bite like every other sibling, and even had a disco light dance-off at home. To avoid getting into trouble when Mom and Dad came back, we quickly cleaned the entire house and made sure there were no signs of our adventures in eating out. It was all in good spirits. Mom and Dad came back the next day and I was leaving for the hostel on the same day.

As I was preparing to depart, I stepped into the restroom to freshen up a bit. However, just as I thought things were settling down, a violent bout of coughing seized me, and this time, something alarming happened—I coughed up blood.

Chapter 5
Happy new year!

When I returned to the hostel, I made another appointment with the doctor, and he reassured me that the blood in my cough might have occurred due to forceful coughing. He advised me to continue with the prescribed medicines and the inhaler. After completing the course of medication, my symptoms improved, but the cough returned the next day. Frustrated with the recurring cough, I decided to consult a different doctor. To my surprise, the new doctor also diagnosed it as a viral cough but adjusted the medication course. With multiple doctors confirming it was viral, I chose to no longer fret over it.

After getting ready, I headed to the concert with Jim. The concert turned out to be an incredible experience. I sang along to the songs, not caring about my less-than-melodic voice. The lights, the band, the confetti, and the sight of everyone's hands in the air created a perfect scene. However, as the concert drew to a close, I was so exhausted that I found a quiet corner to sit in before the event was over. My body was overcome with fatigue, and all I wanted was to get home quickly and sleep. I got back home, took a painkiller, and quickly fell asleep. All this while, I continued my regular workouts, spending over a month consistently exercising at the gym or through brisk walks. My aim was to build strength in my body, but surprisingly, I started feeling more fatigued after each workout, sometimes even experiencing breathlessness. Climbing the stairs to the hostel felt as strenuous as running a marathon. Thinking that yoga might offer a solution, I gave it a try for fifteen days. Unfortunately, the fatigue and cough persisted, and the pain in my upper left back began to intensify. It felt as though the pain was radiating through my left arm. I couldn't sleep the entire night, and any attempt to eat resulted in severe coughing, occasionally leading to vomiting.

At this point, I decided it was time to consult specialists at a renowned hospital rather than local doctors. The next day, I found myself alone without Ishika, who had gone home for some errands, and Vaya was also unavailable. I made my way to the hospital, my cough worsening with every passing minute. In the hospital, I underwent various medical procedures and waited anxiously with an appointment slip in hand. Finally, after what felt like an eternity, my turn arrived. The doctor conducted a spirometry test, which revealed that my lung function was operating at only 20%. The doctor suspected some form of lung infection and even raised concerns about COPD, although it was not confirmed. He diagnosed me with a severe obstruction and prescribed a 15-day course of medication. He also suggested a CT scan after 15 days to get a more comprehensive view.

I called my dad to reassure him and told him not to worry, emphasizing that I had my studies to focus on and that I believed things would improve as I completed the medication course. However, my mom wasn't satisfied with this decision. She scolded me and insisted that I return home immediately. She wanted me to receive a thorough evaluation in our hometown, recover completely, and only then return to my hostel. So, I decided to return home.

During the train ride home, I had a restless night, experiencing persistent fatigue, a headache, and a body ache. I was unable to sleep, and I called my dad around midnight. Despite the late hour, my dad managed to arrange for the necessary medicines to be delivered to me at an unknown train station where my journey had a brief stop. The next morning my parents picked me up from the station.

As we hurried to our family doctor with the spirometry test reports and the prescribed medicines, he expressed some doubts about the diagnosis. To clarify the situation, he recommended further tests and an X-ray. When the X-ray results came in, the doctor called my dad and suggested a CT scan because the left side of the lung wasn't visible in the x-ray. On the same day, we underwent the CT scan, and when we returned to the main doctor with the results, he asked me to wait outside while inviting only my dad in. At that moment, I sensed that something was wrong. When my dad came out, he was teary-eyed, and when I inquired, he didn't say much. As we returned home, my mom pressed my dad for details, and he revealed that there was a tumor in my left lung, and the doctor thought it was pretty serious. We were advised to go to the best hospital possible.

My parents were in tears, and even Bhumi was scared. I, on the other hand, had no idea what was going on but could hear my parents crying as I stood outside the room, trying to eavesdrop a little. Personally, I didn't feel it was that serious, but there was nervousness until we reached the hospital, which was 10 hours away from our home. My health was deteriorating; I couldn't eat anything and was throwing up every hour. Doctors gave me painkiller injections so I could endure the 10-hour journey to the hospital. Unfortunately, the injections didn't seem to help, and even our train got delayed by 5 hours.

Somehow, we reached the hospital in the morning. It was New Year's when my life turned upside down, and I had no idea what to expect. I was admitted to the hospital for the next twelve days.

Chapter 6

Sometimes, the hardest part isn't the diagnosis, but the uncertainty of what's to come.

Life has a way of throwing random lemons at you, and it can take some time to figure out what to do with them. Something quite similar occurred in my life, except instead of lemons, I was handed cancer. A few days ago, I was having an absolute blast on a trip, dancing and screaming my heart out at a concert, with those hip wristbands they hand out. But in the blink of an eye, I found myself in a hospital bed, facing a rare and uninvited guest– lung cancer, that too of a rare type. This time, there were no cool wristbands, just the sterile ones, hospitals give out.

The reasons for why I ended up with it are still a mystery, and I guess they'll forever remain that way. I can still vividly recall the moment when the doctors walked into the room and dropped the bombshell, "We need to kick off chemotherapy as soon as possible." All I could do was stare at that wristband on my hand, thinking, "Huh?" because it hit me so suddenly. It took me a while to wrap my head around everything, to get my thoughts straight. For two months, I'd been told by several doctors that my persistent cough was just a viral thing and that nagging pain in my upper left back was dismissed as a strain due to calcium deficiency. Oh, and the earache in my left ear had nothing to do with those headphones. Turns out, all along, it was Cancer.

The doctors stepped outside and started talking to my dad, but I didn't bother to ask what they were saying. My mom was terrified and just kept crying and praying. Perhaps it's because she'd been down this road before, enduring the pain herself three years ago. Now, knowing her daughter would have to face it too, was shattering her heart.

On the other hand, I felt a wave of overwhelming emotions because I thought I was about to lose everything with this treatment. I feared falling behind everyone else, unable to achieve my goals within the expected timeline, and that was a tough pill to swallow. Cancer didn't even cross my mind at first; I was convinced it wasn't that serious and I'd bounce back to my normal life in six months or a year.

But it hit me like a ton of bricks, and I began to feel anxious about the prospect of losing it all—my hair, my exams, and in my frustration, maybe even friends and relationships. I began to overthink everything, and it became overwhelming. When I saw my dad, I hugged him tightly and burst into tears, unable to hold back. He was crying too, a sight I'd never seen before. My career was my concern; I was already running late, and now with treatment in the picture, I feared I wouldn't be able to take my exams. The life I had when I was away from home in a hostel, wondering if I'd ever get it back, gnawed at me from within.

It came as a shock to everyone. Even after pouring my heart out to my parents, I still felt this immense weight on my chest, as if someone had placed a huge boulder there. So, I instinctively reached for my phone and found messages from Ishika, Kyra, Jim, Adi, and Vaya.

Ishika texted, "This is so sudden, are you okay?"

I replied, almost on the verge of tears, "No, I'm not okay, but I will be."

Ishika continued texting, "Listen to me now, no matter what it is, I'm here for you always. You'll get through this, and one day, you'll write a book about how you overcame it. I'm one hundred percent sure."

Tears welled up in my eyes, and I struggled to find the words to respond. I did not doubt that Ishika would always be there for me, but I had my doubts about the book part. Here I was, still processing the cancer diagnosis, and it would take time. I didn't think I'd ever be able to write a book; just getting through it was enough.

Ishika passed me Vaya's message too. I couldn't reach Vaya since she was abroad with her family on vacation. Her message read, "I am coming to see you as soon as I get home, miss you." I missed Vaya.

Shortly after, I received a video call from Bhumi. She was home alone, and it was evident she was trying to hold back tears. I didn't say anything right away, and she eventually shared that Kyra had come to visit her, bringing sandwiches. Just having Kyra there made her feel better and alleviated her anxiety. I couldn't have been more thankful for that.

I felt an overwhelming urge to cry, but I didn't want to do it in front of Mom and Dad. So, I slipped into the bathroom, stared at myself in the mirror, and contemplated how I would look without hair. I was more concerned about losing my hair at that moment, completely unaware of the pain that chemotherapy would bring. If I had known, I would have realized how trivial my worries about baldness were.

Then, I received a notification from Jim that said, "Are you there? Whatever it is, just let it out."

It struck me that Jim and I had only recently started dating, and it had only been five months. It was clear that it would take some time for me to return to the hostel, and with the treatment and everything, I wouldn't be able to see him. It would be a long-distance relationship, and whenever we discussed it, we concluded that there was no point in continuing a long-distance relationship for an uncertain period. So, we both agreed that if we ever ended up in different places with no idea when we'd be in the same city again, it would be better to end things on a positive note. Maybe that was it.

"I don't know. It's a lot to process, and I have no idea when I'll be back. The whole situation is just so uncertain. I can't be selfish enough to ask you to stay. Also, I don't want to give you any false hope that I'll return soon. To be honest, I'm terrified of losing you in this process. I'm not pushing you away, and I don't know how you'll react, but I couldn't keep it from you," I replied to Jim, tears streaming down my face, without hesitation.

"I understand," Jim replied.

I continued typing, "Everything happened so suddenly. I'm confused, and I have no clue what I should do."

Jim's response came swiftly, almost as if he had already known what to say. He replied, "Let's get this crystal clear. I'm scared, probably more than you are. And if you're searching for reasons why I might feel down, it's not even one percent because I'm concerned about where this will take us or our relationship. Whether it takes you months or a year, whether we end up together or not, whether you see me as your boyfriend, friend, brother, or customer service, the point is I genuinely am not concerned. One thing I'm certain of is that I'm here with you. I'm not leaving you alone in this. And I'm not doing this out of guilt, duty, or some relationship label; I'm doing it because I want to stay. I know you've got a lot on your plate right now, but I don't want you to worry about me. Even if you can't talk to me for a day or two due to treatment, I'll be right here, waiting, and I won't leave, no matter what. Why are you even thinking in that direction?"

"Because I'm afraid I'll end up losing everything," I replied, my tears flowing.

Jim reassured me, saying, "Here's one thing I can promise. I won't promise there won't be arguments or that I'll always be available, but regardless of whether the world stays or walks away, I'll stand by your side…

Chapter 7

If it's hard, you're probably growing.

I was quite relieved after that. But still, thoughts kept flowing into my head so fast that I couldn't think straight. So, I decided to sleep over it.

I was not scared of the diagnosis because, three years back, I saw my mother go through cancer, and that was more difficult. So, I thought if she can recover completely, I will be fine. I was worried that I would fall behind.

I was so preoccupied with worrying about the wrong things that I failed to grasp the one thing that truly mattered – my health.

The entire process of being diagnosed with cancer, going through biopsies, and everything in between had me on edge. The biopsy was especially nerve-wracking. The doctor was about to give local anesthesia, and before he even started, I burst into tears out of fear. Looking back, that was probably the easiest part of the whole ordeal. The only time I teared up during any of the procedures was because, from then on, I mentally toughened myself for whatever was on the horizon. I steeled myself for whatever challenges lay ahead, and once I did that, things became a bit easier because I was mentally prepared. There was a lot of nervousness throughout, but I knew that I would get through it.

It was the moment when I first realized that we often make things seem more daunting in our minds than they truly are. We tend to overcomplicate things mentally when we can simplify them.

Doctors had doubts that it was cancer even before the biopsy. They asked me questions like if I heard wheezing sounds while breathing, if I felt breathless, or if I coughed up blood. My answer was "Yes" to all of their questions. Biopsy results would take two to three days to come out. Those three days are etched in my memory. I was still chilling, watching TV, eating whatever junk and delicious food I wanted. The hospital was good in that way.

There was nagging anxiety and a strange overwhelming feeling in my chest. I couldn't exactly pinpoint the reasons, but I guess I was worried about the results. As soon as they came out, doctors decided to start chemotherapy.

But before that, they needed to fit a PICC line in my right hand. A PICC line, which stands for Peripherally Inserted Central Catheter, is a long, thin tube inserted through a vein in your arm and passed to the larger vein near your heart. It provides access to the large central veins near the heart and is generally used for administering medications.

Doctors couldn't fit the chemo port near the neck area, which is usually under the skin, and fitted through surgery. It's less prone to infections and blood clots compared to the PICC line, but it wasn't an option for me because I had a tumor there.

The next day, they wheeled me into the operating theater. It wasn't a massive room, but the doctor and nurses were busy preparing everything they needed for the PICC line insertion procedure.

I was a bit scared because I knew there would be four cuts and stitches in my arm, and that long, thin tube was going to be inserted. However, I held my tears back as they got me ready. To distract me, the doctors kept talking to me throughout the procedure. They were giving me local anesthesia in my arm and four painful injections to numb the area for the PICC line insertion and stitches. I could still feel some of it happening, though.

I didn't dare to look, but it felt like my arm was a piece of cloth being stitched. The whole procedure took about 15 minutes. They told me I'd need to change the dressing every week, which worried me because I have sensitive skin. I was trying to distract my mind this whole time by thinking about some funny reels on Instagram or any such incidents that are close to my heart. I believed I could fool my anxiety and fear. It did help though, a little.

When I came out of the operating theater, I saw my mother, who had probably been praying the whole time that I wouldn't come out crying like I did during the biopsy. Instead, she had this big smile on her face, as if she had won something big when she saw me coming out cheerful and smiling. My dad hugged me, and the whole family was there, waiting outside the operating theater, even though it wasn't allowed. I felt like I was now prepared for anything. I wasn't feeling as anxious as I was two to three days before.

Mom told me that she got calls from Ishika and Kyra, checking if I was doing fine. I picked up my phone and saw a text from Adi.

The text read, "Hey bbyg, stay strong and keep giving updates. Give me a call whenever you are free."

"Yeah, love you," I replied as they wheeled me back to my room.

I finally received over ten messages from Vaya, which read, "Hey, how are you? I just reached the hotel. I hope you are doing fine. If you'd like, I will spam you with good pictures, sunset pictures, as you like it, to keep you entertained in the hospital. See you soon."

She sent me some of the most beautiful sunset pictures, and it was so pleasant to see them. I replied, "Hey, keep spamming me, I need it. Miss you."

After that, I had my lunch. The thought of starting chemotherapy tomorrow was making me a bit anxious, but I was determined and grateful that I was receiving treatment from the best hospital possible. Because of my family's previous experience with my mother's cancer, my dad was well-informed about hospitals, doctors, and procedures.

So, I was taken care of like a newborn baby. The whole night after the PICC line insertion was painful due to the stitches, and I couldn't sleep. I tossed and turned in pain until midnight when I finally called the doctor because it hurt too much. He gave me a few painkiller injections, and after shedding two or three tears,

I closed my eyes, constantly chanting, "I am stronger than this, I am stronger than I think I am," in my head. My dad sat beside me on a chair near my bed, gently tapping my head to help me fall asleep. After that, I had a good night's sleep.

When I woke up in the morning, I saw my mom sitting beside me. I could tell that my parents took turns sitting by my side during the night, just in case I woke up or needed anything. I felt bad because they hadn't slept properly because of me.

My thoughts were filled with concern, particularly for Bhumi. My friends had kindly been checking on her too. Bhumi is quite introverted, rarely confiding in anyone other than me and her best friend from school, not even our parents. She cared for me so much that she didn't want to burden me with her trauma, so she didn't cry much in front of me. I was concerned about her because, as a child, seeing our mom go through cancer and now me, it's a lot to handle. But she was doing surprisingly well, trying to lighten the mood with her silly yet funny jokes.

The doctors and nurses entered the room abruptly, signaling the start of the chemotherapy. The entire chemotherapy process was going to take eight to ten hours to complete. The medications they were giving me were probably the strongest available, with no higher dosage in my case.

Several saline pre-medication bottles were set up to mitigate potential nausea, fatigue, and acidity, among other issues. In addition, there were two sizable bottles of chemotherapy drugs and two smaller saline flush bottles, likely intended to prevent blood clots in the PICC line. To distract myself, I tried to imagine them as juice bottles, despite their less-than-pleasant taste. I needed to be vigilant for any signs of unbearable breathlessness or other side effects once the chemotherapy drugs were introduced.

As the chemotherapy commenced, it felt as though it was draining every ounce of energy from my body. My strength was nearly depleted, and I couldn't even shift my position in bed without assistance. I had to rely on someone to help me. Breathing became a challenge, and my thoughts grew hazy. The medical team paused the chemotherapy for a quarter-hour, administered a nebulizer to help me breathe properly, and then resumed the chemotherapy at a slower pace.

While the chemotherapy continued, I kept affirming to myself, "These chemo drugs are healing me, my body is accepting them and getting better than ever." Although it was hard to believe at that point, I held onto hope.

In retrospect, it was all that I needed, hope. Hope is what will get you through, no matter how impossible it may seem.

It's much easier to talk about than to put into action – holding onto hope and counting your blessings when it seems like your life is crumbling. I've felt the same way, but it wasn't during my cancer treatment; I experienced it when I watched my mom go through treatment three years ago. It's that overwhelming sense of helplessness that engulfs you, knowing there's nothing you can do to alleviate your loved one's pain. You're left with no choice but to sit by their side and witness their suffering. But believe me, I'll keep on saying it – there's always something to be grateful for.

I was thankful that my dad was strong, decisive, and financially capable of providing my mom and me with the best possible treatment. I was also grateful for my mom's unwavering determination to face it all. It all comes down to your mindset.

The initial round of chemotherapy was complete. The unease of stepping into the unknown lingered, prompting a two-day stay at the hospital for observation and an injection to manage my WBC count. My vitality had dwindled, and I felt restless and nauseous. Nurses came in for the stomach injection, evoking a momentary panic that subsided as I practiced steady breathing. Upon returning home, nausea persisted, making the journey a tumultuous one.

Yet, amidst it all, a strong mental resolve kept me pushing forward. After about 10-15 days in the hospital, coming home brought a sense of relief. However, the next two weeks proved to be an arduous ordeal — fatigue, vomiting, constant nausea, palpitations, mouth sores, skin reactions to the PICC line dressing, constipation, and more.

During this time, I maintained a diary for affirmations, jotting down positive thoughts whenever my health allowed. Gratitude and affirmations shielded me from unnecessary fear and doubt. I firmly believed in the healing power of my body, envisioning a radiant light in my chest shrinking the tumors.

Determined not to succumb to doubt or unnecessary internet searches, I focused on the treatment's positive trajectory. Mistakes were made initially, but I quickly learned the futility of dwelling on uncertainties.

It was clear in my head that doubting treatment and searching deep on the internet about the disease and medicines was useless.

I initially made that mistake but was lucky enough to learn that it was a waste of time. You just give an invitation to futile thoughts, and it hampers your composure by injecting fear. After undergoing fifteen days of chemotherapy, my hair began its silent descent, leaving traces on pillows, in the bathroom, and entwined in the brush.

What commenced as a stray strand or two soon escalated into a cascade of falling locks. With each hair loss, I felt a heaviness in my chest and fast heartbeats. I tried cutting it short, but that didn't help, so I decided to shave my head. Surprisingly, I felt a sense of relief afterward. It wasn't entirely comfortable, but I convinced myself that, with time, it might get better.

I remember having a chat with Kyra about manifestation and affirmations, where she asked me to write to the point and precise affirmations with date, time, result, and everything. So, according to that, I started framing my affirmations. I had my PET scan after three chemotherapy cycles to see if my body was supporting the chemotherapy drugs or not. I already believed that the chemo drugs were healing me.

But Kyra said I framed a few precise and practical affirmations, one of which was, *"I have my PET scan in a month, on 26th March, the results are out the next day and are exceptional. There's almost 60-70 percent recovery already."*

I started believing it with all that I had, no matter the outer circumstances, and to my surprise, the results were out, and my body was reacting positively to the drugs with a significant reduction in the size of the tumor from 10.0 x 7.5 cm to 5.0 x 2.5 cm. Doctors were glad to see the positive results as they were unsure of it earlier.

My parents' happiness had no boundaries. Now, it might be a coincidence, you think, the affirmation and the results, and you might be right as well. But the point is not the affirmation but the positive outlook that it gave me and kept me away from stress and futile thoughts that is important.

These positive results gave me confidence, and I understood that it is important for me to keep my mental health in check. Any kind of stress on my body and mind could hamper my health and recovery. So, I started doing things that I enjoy, learning new and fun skills maybe. A few months back, I was in a rat race, worrying about my career and social life and the pressure of living life to the fullest along with all of these hindrances. But suddenly I was thrown out of that race. To be honest, it used to hit me a lot when I would see what people of my age were doing, and here I was in the hospital dealing with unexplainable pain. I used to get angry at times and would start thinking about where I went wrong. But there were no answers to any of these. I would often run to my dad's precept diary, and even there, things would go bouncer as I couldn't relate to any of it.

Now, looking back, I realize that the diary had all the answers; I just needed to ask the right question. I was happy to have come halfway. It was just a matter of three more chemotherapy cycles. But a lot was going to change after that, and I was completely unaware. I was in a rush to complete these six cycles of chemotherapy, and in a few months, I could get back to normal. I was so wrong.

Chapter 8

When you're lost in the dark, keep your heart tuned to the stars.

The days after the side effects of chemotherapy subsided would go pretty fast. Then the time for the next chemo cycle would come. And all the pain that I went through during the first cycle, I used to get flashbacks of that. And I would feel nauseous and anxious a day before my chemo cycle. I did not fight that feeling.

But I had bigger goals in front of me, so I held tightly on to the thought that, "This too shall pass" and it's just a matter of three chemotherapy cycles. In no time, I would get back to my health. What helped me navigate through a situation like this was my strong desire to live and to feel okay.

I had immense faith in the body's healing powers. Having my parents and Bhumi around all the time to take care of me provided constant moral support. I was fortunate to have people around me who, no matter what, would keep a check on me and were just a text away.

They witnessed countless rants, cries, frustration, and more. In situations like these, it's crucial to keep your loved ones close.

With genuine people, you'll notice that nothing is forced—love, care, and support all come naturally.

They stick around, offering happiness and peace, no matter how challenging the situation becomes.

Despite exams approaching in the next three months, I started contemplating how I could prepare without compromising my health.

Passing the exam wasn't my primary goal; I aimed to do whatever was possible, and even attempting the exam was sufficient. With a PICC line inserted in my right hand, I practiced writing whenever I felt well enough, ensuring that during the exam, I could write for three hours without straining or experiencing pain.

Fatigue hindered me from completing daily tasks, and attempting to push myself resulted in deteriorating health until late at night. Eventually, I learned to be patient with my body, avoiding overexertion. While there were moments of anxiety initially, I stopped making a list of tasks and focused on the next hour, taking breaks or napping when needed. Some days I could study, while others required complete rest. All I could think about was how I would set everything right once I emerged from this phase.

Numerous changes occurred, and though I accepted my cancer diagnosis, accepting the changes that came with it was more challenging. Weight gain due to steroids and drugs, something I had been conscious of since childhood, became difficult to accept suddenly. Gradually, I realized I had lost interest in my appearance, and it no longer mattered to me.

After my fifth chemotherapy session, relief flooded over me, and tears of joy welled up in my eyes. The thing I had been waiting for so long was finally here; I just had to hold on a little longer.

The time for my sixth and final chemotherapy arrived, and I knew that even though the chemo cycles were ending, there would still be a need for ongoing treatment or monthly checkups.

Nonetheless, I was happy that the most challenging part was behind me—no more grappling with side effects. After the last chemotherapy, doctors scheduled the next PET scan to determine further treatment based on its results. The side effects of chemo gradually subsided within four to five days, and I began planning how to regain my strength, considering my body had been fatigued from six cycles of chemotherapy.

The day of the PET scan came, and the results were out the next day. The wait for the results was full of what-ifs. But I was grateful enough to have received the positive results. All the tumors in my body were dissolved completely, as I was told. Dad and I went to the main doctor with the reports. Seeing the result, he said, "Exceptional recovery." Dad, being concerned about my health and future, asked if it would recur in the future.

To which the doctor said, *"Cannot give a guarantee of anything as she was in the fourth stage, but as she has responded well to the treatment, let's hope for the same in the future as well."*

I was unaware of the stage. Sooner, I found out that I had been given six months of life expectancy if chemotherapy didn't work.

Everything was hazy. The doctors were saying something, but I couldn't understand anything. I was tearing up. Suddenly, all the noises in the background were silent, and I could hear my heartbeats. Though the doctor was saying that I was out of danger now, the fact that I was going to die terrified me.

Until then, I didn't realize the uncertainty of life. I was completely unaware and stuck with how to deal with this uncertainty. I found myself trapped in the nest of overthinking that I couldn't get out of.

Until I could fully process everything, the doctor decided to put me on maintenance chemotherapy for six cycles. Finishing one round of chemo only to find out there were more ahead was a bitter pill to swallow. In what felt like the blink of an eye, I found myself in the operating theatre for chemo port surgery. The doctor explained that removing the PICC line and installing the chemo port was more practical since the stitches of the PICC line had come undone five times, each time requiring restitching at the same spot.

It was exhausting and frustrating. The day of the chemo port surgery was particularly challenging. I remember being woken up by one of the doctors afterward. It felt like I had been in a deep slumber, but as soon as I stirred, the pain near my chest and collarbone began creeping in. My body felt utterly drained; I barely had the energy to move. I was parched but wasn't allowed to drink water immediately after the surgery. I kept throwing up, and with stitches near my neck and collarbone, I felt so fragile, like I was on the verge of passing out. The doctors reassured me that I would feel better in a week, but the very next day, I had another chemotherapy session.

Just when I thought things might ease up, they became fifty times harder. That week was one of the most grueling, both physically and mentally. By the time I got home, I had missed my exams and was overwhelmed by the chemotherapy side effects, coupled with a persistent sense of anxiety that left me feeling numb and hopeless.

During the first two or three months of treatment, I took complete rest. But after that, I decided it was time to develop a hobby. I was clueless at first, struggling to figure out what I enjoyed, until I revisited my childhood memories to uncover long-forgotten hobbies. I decided to pick up the keyboard and guitar again, and I even started painting. I wasn't much of a reader, but I resolved to build a habit of reading as well. Since I couldn't take exams, I thought of learning new skills instead.

At first, these activities gave me a sense of purpose, but that feeling only lasted about a month. Soon, frustration began creeping back. There were days when, without any specific reason, I would break down in tears, sometimes six or seven times in a single day, even during periods when there were no chemo side effects. For eight or nine days after each chemotherapy session, the side effects would hit with full force, leaving me bedridden. The fatigue was so intense that even moving a finger felt unbearable. For two or three days out of those nine, the pain was excruciating to the point where even the touch of a pillowcase against my skin was agonizing.

I would force myself to get up and eat, but the constant sensation of nausea made it almost impossible to hold anything down. At times, I would sit in the bathroom for an hour after throwing up, too drained to move. I'd push myself to return to bed, where I would lie motionless, feeling like all the positivity, affirmations, and good thoughts I had tried to cultivate had completely evaporated.

This cycle repeated every 21 days, no matter how much I mentally prepared myself each time. Each cycle felt just as torturous as the last. There were moments when the pain was so unbearable that I would either wish to pass out or beg to be sedated. During the first six chemotherapy cycles, I held onto the hope that the treatment would end and life would return to normal. But then the doctor mentioned 12 maintenance chemo cycles and admitted he couldn't guarantee how many I would need; it all depended on the PET scans. Even after the chemotherapy ended, frequent hospital visits would remain part of my routine.

I kept reminding myself that my body was recovering, that I just needed to hold on for a little longer. But how long was I supposed to wait? I realized that if I wanted to live a fulfilling life, I couldn't keep waiting for the "right time." I had to start living, even amid the chaos.

There were traumatic moments so vivid that they would haunt me long after they'd passed, giving me shivers even weeks later. Though I told myself I had accepted my circumstances, a part of me still longed desperately to return to the life I once had—to the hostel, to the freedom of going wherever I wanted without worrying about my health. I missed the days when I could go to aerobics classes, but now, even jumping was forbidden because of the strain it would put on my bones after the weight I had gained. Scrolling through old photos would often break my heart.

I felt stuck, unable to fully let go of the life I desperately wanted back. The question that plagued me was: how was I supposed to accept this completely? How could I let go of something I still yearned for with all my heart? I didn't have an answer.

When the doctor mentioned 12 more chemo cycles, I felt like the universe was conspiring against me. But even as tears rolled down my face, I knew deep inside that I was a fighter. I decided to write my story—not just to document everything I had endured but as a reminder never to take my health for granted again. I didn't know how or what I would do with my life, but I was determined to make something good out of it. That thought wasn't just an idea anymore; it became my belief. And when a thought transforms into belief, the path to fulfilling it reveals itself.

A week later, when my health stabilized, I decided to work on my writing skills. Within a month, I met the best mentor I could have ever asked for. On our very first day, he asked me, "You seem good at writing, so why do you need someone to teach you?" His words struck me deeply: this was my story, and I should be the one deciding how it should unfold.

I had spent years believing that I couldn't express myself well. Yet here was someone who believed in me before I could believe in myself. He challenged me to come up with a name for my book within a week. Impatient as I am, I came up with the name and even wrote the first page within a day.

Overthinking and self-doubt often hold us back, but you have to start somewhere. Sorting through the chaos in your mind is a necessary process. For me, I knew I had to walk into my next chemo session with a stronger mindset, no matter what it took.

That's where my journey of self-growth truly began.

Chapter 9
Fear of death

The first step was to sort things out in my head—exactly what thought was affecting me so much. The first thing that came to mind was the 'fear of death.' Even though I was out of danger and all the tumors had dissolved, not all, really; a small 1 cm tumor near the collarbone was still there.

I knew by then that merely venting to someone was not a solution, and the more I ran away from this fear, the more it would haunt me.

So, I started contemplating and realized that anyone facing illness, the struggle for life, or the loss of a loved one is well aware of life's unpredictability.

People often associate serious illnesses like cancer with an upcoming date with the Grim Reaper, but they overlook the universal truth that everyone, whether they're sick or not, young or old, is playing the same game of cosmic roulette. That fear goes with the complete acceptance of this truth. Now, you might think of it as impractical.

How is someone supposed to accept the fear of death? By understanding that it is something that is not in your control and thinking about it, stressing over it is not going to let you live in the now. If you start noticing your thoughts consciously, then you will realize that you are stressing either over the future or crying over the past, which is not letting you live in the present. I realized this, but the question was how to live in the present.

By taking one day at a time—and hear me out, it's not easy at first. Learning the art of taking one day at a time is imperative. This is the one mantra that has kept me sane throughout. There are cases and people who were sent home from the hospitals, now there's no cure as they were in the last stage, but still got out of it and are living a healthy and happy life now. Definitely because of the doctors and medicines, but also because of the mindset. We tend to give up on this because we expect immediate results.

We read about changing our mindset and get motivated and expect it to change overnight, yet again we are back to square one the next day. Knowing something is one thing and implementing it is another thing. And implementation is what you should strive for.

I was left with no other option than to think about today. Many futile worries about the future at times used to trigger my anxiety so much that I could see it affecting my health as well. So, a smart choice was to learn to live in the present. I gradually started learning to count my blessings rather than counting on all the stuff I was lacking. If fear of death was something that was scaring me, I started being grateful for waking up each day in the morning.

At first, as I started it, I felt it was useless, but gradually, as months passed, being grateful started coming to me naturally; the lingering anxiety about it was no more. And it's not that I don't get these scary thoughts, but now I started to recognize it as just a thought.

And a thought can be changed. If fear of falling behind everyone due to cancer and treatments was something that I was fretting over, I first threw away all the plans that I had made for the future and started doing things that were possible today without daydreaming about the results I could get out of it. I was scared at first, scared of imagining the future, but rather than focusing on how nice it would be, I started focusing on how I could work on myself today so that I would get a life better than I had imagined.

How can I make myself so strong that I could face any storm? And that is the only thing that is in your control: working on your mind. I slowly and gradually started taking care of my physical and mental health, making it my first and foremost priority. I started making decisions around my health because that is the most important thing in today's date.

I received a rather strong jolt in the form of cancer, which made me truly appreciate the value of my health. We take our health for granted until we lose it.

I read a beautiful quote by Zach Sobiech: "You don't have to find out you are dying to start living."

It just takes one thought to look at any situation differently.

First step: Realize that it is just a thought.

Second step: Change it with another productive thought.

Third step: Plan your next hour rather than planning a year. Have goals about your dream life, but be flexible enough if life wants to offer you more than that, and if that means becoming your best version by going through the worst, so be it.

Fourth step: Keep doing this continuously, and you will notice that the intensity of that scary thought is getting less.

And as soon as I started to look at it this way, I was relieved. The anxiety that was nagging for so long would go away with this realization.

The second thing that was troubling me was my impatience. This impatience of finishing off treatment and then starting to live a new life was the biggest hindrance. I was passing my days looking at the clock. I would get upset, and I would compare it with people.

Now, dealing with the comparison that was so inbuilt for many years—how to deal with that? Realize that "Everybody has their own unique timeline." It's all in our heads. Competition and comparison are good until they're healthy.

The moment it starts stressing you out, you should know where to stop and snap out of it, and it can be done when you understand this one simple thing: Time is a real thing, you just need to have immense faith in yourself that you'll do something good with your life.

Going through the chemotherapy, I always desperately waited for the right time to come when everything was okay, and I was healthy again and in the perfect shape that I wanted to be. That hurry of having my imagined perfect life somehow made me more anxious and unhappy with what I am currently. I was somewhere failing to understand the magic of time and how important it is to be patient. I have this theory or belief that time is never wrong. In whatever situation you are today, you are at the right place at the right time.

The only thing is how you take it. I mean, if the situation is a happy situation, we accept it without any question. The problem comes when the situation that we are going through is painful. In that case, you have choices. If you can do something about it, then do it; but if you can't, if it seems out of your control, you need to be patient and have hope.

This takes immense self-care, and you will keep failing at it at first, which I did. But I just started thinking that this period of my life is the toughest period, and if I learn to live my life while going through cancer treatment, if I learn to hold onto myself and hope for the best, if I start thinking of it as what this period has taught me rather than thinking that what it has taken away from me, if I start creating and working towards the best version of myself rather than losing myself, then I will be able to get through any situation in the future.

I remember my old self, or the girl I was before the cancer diagnosis. If you'd asked that girl if she would survive the situation she's going through right now, she would have said no. But here I am, getting through everything I thought I never would. And I even want you to think of the worst thing that you have been through and ask yourself the same.

I would like to remind you that if you can get through that, you can get through anything. You just need to have that faith in yourself and in time as well, because time heals everything. If time has taken away from you something, have faith that it will heal you. Nothing stays forever. When it seems that you can't bear the pain, hold onto this thought that nothing stays forever. It will make you angry at times, frustrated even, but you have no option but to keep reminding yourself.

When I am going through chemotherapy, it feels as though I keep trying to remind myself of all of what I have said above. It feels like somebody is dragging me back to square one, back to where I am miserable.

I even end up getting these thoughts that what is the point of living like this, that there's no zest left to live and that I am tired in pain constantly, and it feels next to impossible to remind yourself of all the positive things. But realize this thing that when you are down physically, when your energy levels are down, you are bound to get negative thoughts sometimes, and that is completely fine. Mental and physical well-being are like a sitcom – they keep the show of life entertaining.

Just imagine waking up with a headache – you'll see how the day can take a turn for the worse if that headache persists. If someone enthusiastically tells you to "be positive" when you're feeling unwell, your first instinct might be to hurl something at them. But here's the million-dollar question: how do you manage to keep your wits about you while dealing with something way more serious than a pesky headache? Let's not sugarcoat it; it's not a walk in the park. But the biggest secret to staying sane, I've discovered, is not to wrestle with your emotions. Release yourself from the pressure of being all sunshine and rainbows when all you feel inside is like the lead character in a melodrama.

It's important to vent it out. There are times in life when everything seems to be falling apart. In situations like these, the worst thing you can do to yourself is to panic and attempt to control everything. So what's the alternative? Trust the timing of the Universe because nothing stays forever. Release the need for everything to be picture-perfect. If you feel like shedding a tear or two, give yourself a little emotional rain shower.

I once read a profound quote in the book "Forest of Enchantments": "What you can't change, you must endure." And that stayed with me.

As I endure the pain of the side effects of chemotherapy, I allow myself to feel every thought that is coming to my head. I cry to my parents, to my sister, to my friends. I allow myself to indulge in self-pity for a while. It is important to let your emotions out because the more you suppress them, the more you will keep storing them, and it will find disastrous ways to get out.

For example, you may have noticed that a person who has spent all his or her young age days, or more than half of their life, being calm is more likely to become a walking volcano in old age. So those 8 to 9 days, I don't put any kind of pressure on myself, but after that, when the side effects subside, I notice that I don't get those negative thoughts so much, then I push myself a little bit to again start working towards the mindset that I am striving for. I felt like some punching bag, getting hit by the chemo every time and bouncing back to normal again after that. It's a cycle of resilience after every 21 days.

But I promised myself to give my best and make the most of those ten to fifteen days of the month where I feel physically a bit better. It took some time to get used to it, but eventually, it became my routine. *I focused one hundred percent on what I could do today.*

Chapter 10

Sometimes, it's not the why that matters, but the will to keep going.

A month ago, I wasn't able to understand why this was happening to me because I was searching for the 'why,' and trust me, there's no answer to why. The only thing you need to do is constantly keep learning. All this while, all I wanted was to get better, but I was focusing too much on cancer. The more and more you keep thinking and reading or listening about the disease, the more you surround yourself with that disease. My thoughts revolved around the fact that I am sick and how I am not able to do what I want because of cancer. But soon I realized that these thoughts are futile.

The more I kept having these thoughts, the more I would dwell on them. So, I started reading books, learning new skills, learning musical instruments, and writing. I found myself happy when I kept doing these things. I decided not to use cancer as an excuse. I decided that I would not let it hold me back. If at times I couldn't read because of all the fatigue in my body, I started listening to audiobooks. The whole day, I was occupied with reading and writing, constantly surrounding myself with all the things I wanted to imbibe in me. Reading and listening to all the stuff that gave me hope. As I started doing this consistently, I started to fall in love with reading books, fiction, self-help books, and human psychology, and when confused, I always had Bm Sir to the rescue to discuss and solve any confusion regarding it.

All the discussions with him slowly and gradually cleared the hazy picture in my mind of how I wanted to live my life. With all the pain, frustrations, and anxiety of treatment, I wanted my life to be happy and content. I had no idea how I was going to do that, but I had this belief that I would make my way through it. I would allow myself to make mistakes and learn from them.

I began searching for people who had endured similar battles, if not exactly like mine, then at least those who had faced sickness in some form. I was yearning for that sense of relatability because, despite being surrounded by people who genuinely cared for me, there were moments I felt profoundly alone.

It wasn't their fault; I simply couldn't find the words to explain the depth of my pain. At times, even I couldn't fully comprehend it—why it was so intense, why it lingered relentlessly. I could only feel it, live it, and that unexplainable torment often left me frustrated and irritable. Yet, I knew one thing with certainty: I couldn't expect anyone—not my family, not my friends—to truly understand what I was going through.

They could sympathize, but the experience was mine alone to bear. Even though I had seen my mother endure chemotherapy, and she had some understanding of the pain, there were still gaps between us, shaped by generational differences in how we processed and felt things.

I made it my goal to feel independent and secure within myself by managing my expectations of others. I didn't want my happiness, or even my sense of normalcy, to hinge on someone else. I wanted to reclaim the parts of me that felt lost amidst this storm.

Chemotherapy had a way of making me feel like my normal life had been pulled away from me entirely. My days became an endless loop between home and the hospital. My parents often took me out to different places, hoping to lift my spirits, but the joy of those outings was overshadowed by my body's limitations. Ten or fifteen minutes of walking would leave me utterly exhausted; the fatigue and body aches would creep in, robbing me of any pleasure in those moments. Most of my time was spent at home, and it began to gnaw at me from the inside.

I reached a point where I was tired—tired of feeling like this, tired of waiting for it to get better. That's when I decided I couldn't let this be my reality anymore. I started seeking ways to shift my perspective and reclaim even the smallest fragments of joy.

I realized that the only person who could truly understand and take care of me was me. It required an immense amount of self-care and determination to work through the frustration, to push past the inertia of pain and exhaustion. I discovered that the key lay in keeping myself engaged, immersing myself in things I wanted to embody. It wasn't easy—some days, it felt almost impossible. The pain would make it tempting to stay in bed and give in to despair. And you know what? That's okay. Those moments of surrender are human.

But here's the thing: you have to give yourself that little push. Just a nudge toward something—anything—that brings even a sliver of light into the darkness. And if you're someone who has a loved one battling cancer, you can be that nudge, that catalyst. My family and friends were my constant cheerleaders, and their support was invaluable.

Still, I've learned something important through it all: at the end of the day, you are enough. Enough to mend the wounds of your heart, enough to find your own strength, enough to navigate the storm. It won't be perfect, and it won't be easy. But you are capable.

My treatment started off in January, and I remember feeling all alone in March after my third chemotherapy, lying in my bed scrolling through Instagram. I came across one girl named Bri who posted a reel that said, "Watch my hair grow back." She seemed young and of my age. After watching that reel, I went through her profile and stalked her for an hour. I could relate to every single thing. I couldn't help myself from sliding into her DMs.

"Hey! I was just scrolling through the feed when I saw your hair regrowth journey video and checked your profile...

I am in the midst of my cancer treatment. I could relate to all of your posts because that's what I am facing currently. I am feeling stagnant and sad sometimes, even exasperated and exhausted. The thought of waking up daily and getting through the day haunts me.

Due to this treatment, I have gained weight, lost all my hair, the pain, and the fact that I can't do anything about it unless I get over the treatment is making me anxious. I don't know you personally, and I don't expect you to see my texts or respond to it, but I hope you get all that you want and more of it. Thanks for doing what you're doing. You've no idea how much it has helped. I still feel helpless, but there's hope."

To which she replied, *"Hey there* ♥

First off, I just wanted to say I'm so sorry you are going through all of that. I know 100% how you feel. And it can be SO hard to not feel like yourself, and I remember having the same feeling of getting through the day scaring me. I promise you with my full heart that this pain goes away. And you will learn so, so, so much. I always hated people telling me that, but it's true. We have a special outlook on life that makes us appreciate it so much. Not many people have that. And I also relate with close ones not understanding what you're going through ♥ *That was so hard for me too. I remember hanging out with my friends, and I would get bothered if they complained about homework. Because in my head, I was like, "ugh, I wish my problems were homework and not cancer." Anyway, I totally get where you're coming from. But as time went on, we are BEST friends again. And I learned to not let those things bother me. I promise you will get past this* ♥ *Keep your hope!!!! Hope is what will get you through. And I don't know if you're religious, but I'm sending lots of prayers your way. And know God cares for you more than anything. He loves you. I love you too! You got this* ♥ *"*

Tears rolling down my eyes as I read the text, and there was a strong positive energy in me, and that was hope. I saw her profile, her journey from not being able to get up from the bed to running 10 miles a day, going to the gym, getting in shape. She was doing everything that I wanted for myself but I was having second thoughts about it. After seeing her and reading her text, I only had hope and kindness in my heart.

Even after going through the worst, she was filled with kindness, love, positivity, and hope. I realized that when you are filled with that kind of energy, you end up radiating the same. And when I feel the lack of hope, I keep going back to her profile and texts.

While going through my 14th chemotherapy, in the period where I hit rock bottom and feel like I cannot take this anymore, and I would feel tired of even having hope at times and feeling completely helpless, I would text

Bm Sir saying, "I am tired now, what if it doesn't get better?"

To which he would reply, *"Then it will be the best."*

"I hope so," I replied, tears rolling down through my eyes.

He would always say, *"You are more than what you think about you."*

I would listen to all the people who have been through sickness. They had negligible chances of living, yet they ended up achieving and living more than they could ever imagine.

I realized that people have recovered from impossible, insane diseases with the power of hope, and all I could think of was, "Why can't I?"

There was a young girl who grew up in a hot Las Vegas desert. All she wanted was to be free and independent. At the age of 19, after she graduated from school, she moved to a place where it snowed and became a massage therapist. With that, she felt free and completely in control of her life—until her life took a detour. She went home from work early one day with what she thought was the flu, until 24 hours later, she found herself in the hospital on life support with less than a 2 percent chance of living.

As days passed, she laid in a coma, and doctors diagnosed her with bacterial meningitis, a vaccine-preventable blood infection. Over the course of two and a half months, she lost her spleen, kidney, the hearing in her left ear, and both of her legs below the knee. When her parents wheeled her out of the hospital, she thought the worst was over—until she saw her new legs for the first time. They were like heavy metal blocks. She did not know what to expect, but she wasn't expecting that. With her mom on her side and tears rolling down their faces, she strapped on those chunky legs. She stood up.

They were so painful and so confining that all she could think of was how she was ever going to travel the world with these chunky legs, how she was always going to live the life full of adventures and stories as she always wanted, and how she was going to snowboard again. She went home, crawled into bed, and that was her situation for a few months—escaping the reality with her legs resting by her side. She was physically, mentally, and emotionally broken. She knew she had to let go of her old version and learn to embrace her new self. That's when it dawned on her that she wouldn't have to be 5ft 5 anymore. She could be as tall as she wanted or as short as she wanted, depending on who she was dating! And if she snowboarded again, her feet wouldn't get cold anymore.

She asked herself a life-defining question: *If your life were a book and you were the author, how would you want your story to go?* She began to daydream and imagine herself walking gracefully, helping other people through her journey, and snowboarding again.

She did not just see herself doing that; she could feel it. And four months later, she was back on the snowboard. Although things did not go as she expected and it was difficult to be able to snowboard again, she was so discouraged. She decided to make a new pair of legs that could fit her right. It was these legs and, her best 21st birthday gift, she received a new kidney from her dad that allowed her to follow her dreams again.

She started snowboarding, went back to work, to school, and in 2005, founded a non-profit organization for youth and adults facing physical disabilities. From there, she got an opportunity to go to South Africa, where she helped to put shoes on thousands of children's feet so they could attend school. The next thing, she won two back-to-back World Cup gold medals, which made her the highest-ranked adaptive female snowboarder in the world. And she is Amy Purdy for you. Her story taught me the power of imagination, how you can make weaknesses your strength.

I also kept going back to this one story that made me believe in the power of hope: the story of Michael Crossland.

Michael Crossland was diagnosed with a rare and aggressive type of cancer—Neuroblastoma. Doctors gave him only a slim chance of survival, saying he wouldn't live beyond his first year. Despite this prognosis, Michael fought this war with sheer determination and the support of his family.

At 11 months old, Michael went through chemotherapy as part of an experimental treatment. The therapy was so potent that it killed one of the other children in the trial, leaving Michael as the sole survivor. Now, despite spending so much of his early life in and out of hospitals, he was determined to live a normal life. He wanted to pursue sports and dreamed of becoming a professional baseball player, which he achieved in his teenage years. He was even selected for the Australian baseball team; however, his career was cut short when health issues resurfaced.

As a young adult, his body began to experience the long-term effects of chemotherapy. He even suffered a heart attack at the age of 18, severe infections, and immune system failure. Despite these setbacks, he chose to focus on blessings rather than his hardships. He adopted a mindset of gratitude and faith, which many of us in this age have forgotten, and believed that every challenge he faced was an opportunity to learn from.

It sounds so true when he said that: *"We all need to remember, through great adversity and great darkness, this is our discovery moment. We do not discover how unfair life is, but rather we discover how powerful we have been created."*

Months back in January, when I was in such a difficult and critical phase, getting diagnosed at the fourth stage, if today I am out of that critical phase and the disease is in control, and my body has shown insane recovery, then my life has purpose. I just need to have patience with the chemotherapy treatment. And with this, I believed in the power of hope and imagination. I started imagining like a kid again. You have to go back to being a kid again.

Lying in bed, I would imagine a golden-colored light healing every part of my body, shrinking every tumor. I would imagine getting better each day. I would imagine achieving everything that I wanted. I would imagine creating something while sitting at home, feeling as if it's happening at this very moment. Allow yourself to be happy in that moment where you'd always wanted to see yourself. Push yourself a little bit more through imagination.

And remember that the brain questions whether miracles could ever happen, but hope believes and makes them happen! It is very important to believe in that power—to believe that your mind and body have immense healing powers.

Chapter 11
Hope is fragile

If there's one thing that kept me going through the hardest days, it was hope. Not the loud, roaring kind of hope that demands to be noticed, but a quiet, persistent belief that tomorrow might be kinder. Hope, for me, wasn't about denying the reality of my struggles. It wasn't about convincing myself that everything would magically get better. Instead, it was about trusting that even amidst the chaos, there were still things worth holding on to.

When my treatments became grueling, and the future seemed uncertain, I clung to small things that sparked hope: the little victories in my day, like being able to eat or smile despite the pain. Hope taught me that even in the darkest times, there is always a flicker of light waiting to be found.

It wasn't easy. There were days when hope felt like a distant star, barely visible in the vast sky of my fears. But I learned that hope doesn't have to be grand or perfect—it just has to exist. It's the thread that keeps us tethered when everything else feels like it's slipping away

I also realized that hope isn't something we have to find outside ourselves; it's something we can create. I started to imagine a version of myself years down the line, stronger, happier, and grateful for every step of this journey. Holding onto that vision helped me keep moving forward, even on days when I wanted to give up.

Hope isn't about pretending that life is always beautiful. It's about believing that the beauty of life lies in its imperfections and challenges. It's about trusting that the storms will pass and that even if the rain doesn't stop, you can still find joy in dancing in it.

In the evening as I sat quietly, my mind racing with thoughts I couldn't make sense of, Bhumi asked me, "Are you okay? You've been so quiet today."

I could feel the weight of everything—my body, my mind, the uncertainty of it all—and I gave her a tired smile, "I'm fine, just... thinking."

She frowned, concerned about etching her face. "About what? You know you don't have to keep everything in."

I took a deep breath, trying to put words to the fear I was feeling, "What if... hope isn't enough? What if it doesn't work this time? What if it's all just... not enough?"

She didn't say anything at first, but I could see her processing, trying to understand. On that she said leave this let us watch this hilarious standup it would light up your mood.

Even while watching, the thought was still lingering in my mind But as I remembered Emily, a woman just 26 years old, diagnosed with an aggressive form of cancer, I realized something profound: her story echoed so much of my own—she held onto hope fiercely, went through every treatment available, and kept believing she could beat it. She even said, "If hope could cure cancer, I'd already be in remission."

But Emily's cancer didn't respond to the treatments. In the end, her body gave up before her spirit ever did. I thought about her often during my own bad days and wondered: If hope couldn't save her, what's the point?

Later that day at night Lying in bed , I stared at the ceiling, my body aching and my mind swirling with fear. *'Why am I holding onto hope?'* I wondered. 'What if it's all for nothing?' But then, a quieter voice—one I barely recognized—answered back. 'What if it's not? What if tomorrow brings something I'll cherish? What if one small moment makes all of this worth it?' I sighed, letting the thought linger. Hope wasn't loud; it didn't promise me a miracle. It simply whispered, 'Try again tomorrow.'

Next day when I woke up I was not feeling well both mentally and physically. Swallowing my meds felt like ticking off another item on my 'survival checklist

As I was sitting and scrolling cause the anxiety of just laying down and doing nothing triggered me, my mother quietly walked in. She must have noticed my pensive look because she sat beside me without saying a word. After a few minutes, I broke the silence.

Do you ever feel like hope is... fragile?' I asked, my voice barely above a whisper.

She looked at me with a soft smile. *'Hope is fragile,'* she said. *'But it's also stubborn. It might bend under the weight of your fears, but it won't break—not as long as you hold onto it.'*

'What if I let go?' I whispered.

She took my hand gently. *'Then I'll hold it for you until you're ready again. You know, when I was going through my treatment, the uncertainty and fear were inevitable. But amidst all of that, there was one thing that gave me the strength to keep going: thinking about you, Bhumi, and your dad. You both were my anchor during those times. You were the source of my hope, and no matter how afraid I was, I knew I had you both by my side.*

I see that same strength in you, my dear. Even in the toughest moments, I know you have that same fire inside you. And remember, we're always here for you. You're my strongest baby, and I have no doubt you'll get through this. Just trust the process. I know it's hard, and I truly understand. I feel it with you, but unfortunately, I can't change what's happening. The only thing I can tell you is that hope will carry you through, and one day, you'll look back and be grateful you held on to that small ray of light."

Sometimes, all we need are those simple, comforting words—ones that make us feel understood and remind us that we are not alone. It's in those moments, when everything feels overwhelming, that a few sentences can become our anchor, lifting us up just enough to keep going.

And It took me a while to realize something important: Hope isn't about controlling outcomes. It's about how you live, even when outcomes don't go your way. Emily's hope didn't "fail" her — it allowed her to smile through her pain, cherish her final moments with her family, and leave behind a legacy of strength.

something shifted in me after watching a video titled *Hold on to Hope*. It was by Jenny, a woman who had faced what seemed like an insurmountable challenge—a terminal cancer diagnosis. As she shared her story, she spoke about the moment her life changed forever. After being told she had only months to live, she was overwhelmed by hopelessness, until she realized that hope wasn't about survival—it was about living fully, no matter what.

Jenny's words stayed with me: *"Moments and choices will either create hope or dissolve it, but your choices will define your life's outcomes."* I could see the power in her journey. She told the story of her son, Gabriel, and how, even in the face of the hardest battles, she chose to take her power back. She didn't let the doctors' dismissive words steal her hope. Instead, she sought out people who uplifted her, people who became "hope makers" in her life.

The way a single phrase can either diminish you or lift you up. I had felt that firsthand. But what Jenny taught me was that we have the power to control how we respond to those words. It's in our hands to choose hope, to link arms with those who help us shine.

When Jenny said, "Hope doesn't just happen, you have to take action," I realized what I had been missing. Hope wasn't passive. It was a decision. And it was that decision that gave me the strength to keep going.

Just like Jenny, I started to see hope differently. It's not just about wishing for a better outcome—it's about making the choice to live with strength, to find meaning in each day, and to surround myself with hope-makers, just as she had. This wasn't about fighting a disease anymore. It was about embracing life, no matter what came next.

Chapter 12

Cancer tested my body, but my family's love empowered my spirit

Hope kept me going, but it wasn't something I carried alone. It was shared, nurtured, and sometimes even reignited by the people closest to me—my family. They weren't just my support; they were the reason I could still find hope, even in the darkest moments. In their quiet strength and unconditional love, I found not just a reason to hope, but a reason to fight.

During this journey, I remember how the smallest of actions made the biggest differences. My family, despite the chaos and challenges, managed to create an environment of love, laughter, and togetherness. One of the most comforting rituals we had was playing endless rounds of Ludo. It wasn't just a game; it was the way of forgetting the chaos for a while and just being happy playing together. Those moments were more than just distractions—they were reminders of what we were fighting for: each other.

We also made it a point to eat together as a family, every single day, no matter how difficult things got. Meals weren't just about food; they were about unity. Sitting around the table with my loved ones gave me a sense of normalcy, a kind of warmth that was hard to come by during this battle. Even when treatments left me drained, that small act of eating together gave me a reason to smile and feel grounded.

Then there were the rides. Bhumi and I often went out on our scooty, just the two of us. It started with me taking her for rides, but as life changed, so did our roles. Bhumi began to take me, her confidence replacing my strength, and yet the love stayed the same. Those rides were more than just trips; they were symbolic of how we grew up together, adapting, supporting, and finding joy in simple things.

As a family, we didn't just go through this journey; we grew through it. Each of us changed in ways we didn't expect. I still remember the day my dad sat me down, his hands trembling as he broke the news to me. He said it was just the first stage, that we'd start chemo and fight it together. But the tears in his eyes gave away the fear he tried so hard to hide. Watching his helplessness made me want to be strong—not just for me but for him.

The chemo sessions were brutal, but my family made it bearable. My dad, who rarely ever took a break from work, would drop everything the moment I called. He'd sit beside me, feed me with his hands, and stroke my head as if I were still his little girl. He cried when I cried, his emotions becoming a silent yet powerful expression of his love. I'd often place my head on his lap, finding solace in his unwavering presence.

It wasn't just him; my mom stood by me through every hospital visit. She cooked my favorite meals and made sure I never felt alone. Bhumi was my light in those dark moments, always finding ways to make me laugh or distract me with silly games and late-night conversations. Together, they built a cocoon of love and care around me, shielding me from the harsh reality of my illness.

When my hair began to fall out, I saw the pain in their eyes, even though they tried to hide it. Dad said I looked beautiful regardless, but I knew how much it hurt him to see me change. He'd buy me anything I asked for—a piano, new furniture for my room—just to see me smile. Playing the piano became my escape, a way to bring joy back into our home, even if only for a little while.

The trips to Dharamshala and Mumbai brought small moments of happiness. I loved exploring the serene surroundings with Dad, talking about life, and pretending, just for a while, that everything was normal. He believed in me more than anyone else, even consulting astrologers and following their advice in the hope of giving me a fighting chance. His faith gave me strength when I felt like giving up.

On our way home one day, I craved tandoori and dal fry, and Dad stopped at a dhaba to make it happen. It was such a small thing, but it brought me so much happiness.

The bond we shared, the sacrifices we made, and the memories we created—these were the things that carried me through. I realize how vital it was to have a loving and supportive environment during such a tough time. It wasn't just about the physical fight; it was about the emotional strength that came from knowing you're not alone.

I realized something during this time: our family became a fortress. It wasn't perfect—there were moments of fear, frustration, and exhaustion—but love poured out in ways I hadn't seen before. To anyone reading this who might not have this kind of environment, I just want to say—don't lose hope. Surround yourself with even one person who cares, who listens, who makes you feel less alone. Because the truth is, you don't have to fight battles alone. And if you're the family or friend standing by someone's side, remember that your presence, your love—it matters more than words can say. BM sir would always say this, "People are not just words, they are emotions. Never hold onto what they say—grasp their emotion."

There were days I wanted to give up, days when the pain felt endless. But then I'd see Bhumi's smile, hear Dad's terrible jokes, watch my mom prepare the yummiest meals and realize—they believed in me, even when I didn't believe in myself.

Every morning, I would make tea and sit with Dad before the chaos of the day began. In those moments, I would share everything about my life in Pune—my friends, my experiences, and even about Jim. I could feel that when I was happy, he was happy too, supporting me and providing everything I needed. Sometimes, I'd sit quietly and wonder, *How will I ever repay them for everything they've done for me?* Or, if not them, who else could have shown me this kind of love and support?

While my family's love was a constant, it wasn't enough to answer the question I kept asking myself: *Who am I when everything else is uncertain?* Their strength surrounded me, but the battle was mine to face. I learned confidence isn't something we inherit from others—it's something we cultivate from within.

Chapter 13

CONFIDENCE is a gift—but it's a battle won in the depths of your own mind.

Confidence is a gift we're all born with. As children, we rarely question our worth. We don't doubt whether we're too much or too little; we simply exist as we are, with joy and curiosity. No one is born insecure or a certain way—confidence is as natural as breathing.

But as we grow, the world starts to whisper doubts into our ears. It tells us to measure ourselves against others, to seek approval, and to mold ourselves into shapes that fit expectations. For me, this journey became tangled with insecurities about my weight, my appearance, and the endless worry of "What will people think?"

Somewhere along the way, though, life tries to shake that belief. We start measuring ourselves by other people's opinions, comparing our journey to theirs, and doubting whether we're on the "right" path.

But confidence isn't something you lose forever. I've learned it's always there, waiting for you to remember it. The truth is: *we are more than our circumstances, our appearance, or even our achievements. We have infinite potential, and that's where confidence begins.*

Life tested this understanding when cancer became part of my story. At first, it felt like the ground beneath me had crumbled. How could I stay confident when my body didn't feel like my own? But then, the lessons I'd learned came back to me. *Confidence isn't tied to how you look or how others perceive you. It's tied to the realization that you are the mind, the time, the creator of your reality.*

Through reflection, I came to see that confidence doesn't mean being unshaken. It means facing the shaking and standing firm in the knowledge that you'll find balance again. It's about accepting change, not resisting it. Cancer didn't take away my confidence; it transformed it. It deepened it, showing me strength I didn't know I had and teaching me that true confidence is rooted in understanding yourself—not in seeking validation from others.

Every day became an opportunity to practice this understanding. To focus on what I could control: my thoughts, my perspective, and the energy I brought into each moment. Confidence isn't a destination. It's a journey back to the self, to the truth that has been with you all along.

Cancer seemed like it might extinguish that light completely. The weight of the diagnosis, the physical changes, the pitying looks from others—all threatened to bury the person that I once was. And yet, even in the darkest moments, there was a flicker of something familiar: the same spark of confidence that I carried as a child, waiting to be rediscovered.

Confidence—it's like a treasure buried deep inside, hidden beneath layers of doubt and fear. Cancer, in its cruel way, forces you to dig deep and confront those layers. It challenges you to stop looking outward for validation and to turn inward, where confidence has been quietly waiting all along.

I realized that it's about embracing imperfection, showing up despite fear, and recognizing your worth even when the world seems to question it. My journey wasn't about returning to the fearless child I once was, but about finding a new kind of confidence—one forged through pain, resilience, and self-acceptance.

Confidence isn't static. It can be lost and found, broken and rebuilt. It's not something others give you—it's something you reclaim for yourself, piece by piece, moment by moment.

But what if you don't know where to begin with your mind? The mind, with all its power, holds the key. But here's the truth: it doesn't come naturally to everyone, and that's okay. Strengthening your mind is a practice, not a one-time revelation.

For those unfamiliar with the mind's potential, start small. The mind thrives on what you feed it. Every thought you entertain becomes a thread in the fabric of your confidence. When doubt or fear rises, don't fight it—observe it. Acknowledge its presence, but don't let it linger. Instead, shift your focus to a single empowering truth: you've endured, you've survived, and even now, you are more resilient than you realize.

On days when it feels impossible to feel confident—when every effort seems futile—remember this: confidence is not about constant success. It's about showing up just like I did for all the guitar lessons, which were only an hour or so, but just getting up and going was the biggest achievement. Reading and learning new things. The days when I felt like, even after trying, I was still failing—when showing up just seemed very difficult. Those are the days when you need to give yourself permission to rest, to lean into your humanity, and to simply be. Some battles aren't won by force but by patience.

To truly strengthen the mind, practice presence. Spend time each day reminding yourself of what's real. Confidence grows from the small moments when you choose to believe in yourself again. It's not a perfect process. Some days will feel heavy, but even on those days, the effort matters. You are building a foundation, brick by brick, for a version of yourself that no challenge can ever break.

I sometimes become hyper-aware of every small change. A new scar. A shift in my posture. And with every change, the question loomed larger: What will people think? Would they see me differently? For a while, it became a constant worry.

I remember a particularly vulnerable time during my treatment when I felt overwhelmed by insecurity. I had gained a significant amount of weight, and the changes in my body made me feel hesitant to let even those closest to me see me like that. In my insecurity, I told my friends that the doctor wasn't allowing visitors.

What I didn't expect was how deeply they understood me. They gave me space for a while, respecting my feelings without question. But soon enough, they began showing up anyway, their presence a quiet yet powerful reassurance that I was loved exactly as I was.

It was in those moments—when they sat by my side, laughed with me, and refused to let my insecurities create distance—that I realized something profound. We are so much bigger than the fears we harbor about ourselves. To those who truly love us, our external changes or perceived flaws don't matter. Their love is constant, unshaken, and unconditional.

That realization elevated my confidence in a way I hadn't experienced before. I began to see that the people who genuinely care for us are the ones who help us weather life's storms. They don't just stand by us—they remind us, in their quiet, steadfast way, that we are enough, exactly as we are.

One night, I found myself feeling like life was passing me by, as if I were stuck in one place while everyone else was achieving their milestones. The weight of it all became too much, and I broke down, crying quietly in the dark.

My sister, who happened to see me at that moment, surprised me with what she said. We weren't the type to have soft, deep conversations—our sibling dynamic was more about teasing than heartfelt talks—but perhaps that's why her words had such an impact.

She sat beside me and, in her no-nonsense way, said, *"I don't think there's anybody who doesn't go in their room and cry every now and then. We only see the face and side they decide to show, but we're all the same—just with different hardships. That's no reason to feel low about yourself."*

Her words were like a lifeline, cutting through my spiraling thoughts and grounding me in reality. It was a reminder that everyone carries their own battles, no matter how perfect their lives might look from the outside. What I was feeling wasn't unique, but that didn't make it any less valid. It simply made me human.

That moment with my sister changed something in me. It reminded me that comparing my struggles to someone else's highlight reel or stories was not just unfair but also unkind to myself. Her words helped me find comfort in the truth that we're all navigating life's ups and downs in our own way, and it's okay to take my time.

And then, just like that, the question, "What will people think?" started to lose its grip on me.

Instead, I found myself asking a different question: *Why does it matter what they think, when I know who I am inside?*

It didn't come in a single moment of clarity, but I began to realize that no one else's opinion of me could ever define my worth—not the way I looked, not the way I was fighting, not the changes I was going through. Only I could decide who I was and what I believed about myself. And the people around me made these thoughts change very quickly.

Ishika, Kyra and Adi were my steady pillars, showing me encouragement and love when I needed it most.

Ishika would often remind me, *"You are stronger than you think. You're more capable than you realize."*

Kyra, with her unshakable belief in me, would say, *"No matter what, I see the warrior in you. Keep going, you're doing amazing."*

Adi, always full of optimism, would joke, *"You're practically invincible, and don't let anyone tell you otherwise!"*

Each word from them—so simple, yet so powerful—wrapped me in warmth and confidence. It made me feel loved and supported in a way I had never fully understood before. Their words were like a light that reminded me I wasn't alone, that I had the strength to keep going, and that I was already enough, just as I was.

The answer to that new question was simple, but it wasn't easy to embrace: *Confidence comes from within.* It isn't something that can be taken from you by someone else's gaze or opinion. It's built from your understanding of yourself, from knowing that no matter what changes on the outside, the essence of who you are remains constant. And with that understanding, no external judgment—no matter how harsh or well-meaning—can ever shake your foundation.

I understood, amidst this treatment, the truth is, the world is always going to have its opinions. But I had a choice: I could either let those opinions control how I felt about myself, or I could trust in the quiet power of knowing who I was beneath it all. The confidence I had been searching for wasn't something that needed to be earned through approval or validation. It was already there, deep inside me, waiting to be remembered.

As I navigated through life's challenges, I began to notice something profound: my confidence wasn't always a solo journey.

Often, it was sparked by observing someone who lived with clarity and purpose. It wasn't because they asked me to emulate them or handed me a set of instructions—it was never about following them.

Instead, it was the way they lived, authentically and unapologetically, that encouraged me to explore the depths of my own potential.

But what I didn't realize at first was how that spark wasn't meant to stop with me. Confidence thrives when it's shared. The same way my friends, my family, and even strangers gave me strength.

Chapter 14
How one mentor in your life can be catalyst of change

It's funny how life works sometimes. You can go years feeling like you're carrying the weight of the world alone, and then, on an ordinary day, someone appears—a stranger who unexpectedly becomes a guide, a mentor, a light in the dark. That's how it happened for me.

I remember the day I decided to seek help. It wasn't a moment of crisis, but a quiet realization that I wanted more for myself.

I wanted to grow, to understand myself. I had read so many books, watched countless videos, and thought I could figure it all out on my own. But something in me knew that I needed guidance—someone who could help me connect the dots and push me further than I could go alone.

That's when I found him. It started with a simple online search, and before I knew it, I was talking to someone who changed the way I perceived life.

When I say he is the best mentor I have ever met, I mean it with all my heart. He didn't just teach me how to handle the challenges that cancer threw my way; he gave me the tools to understand my mind. Through our discussions—sometimes deeply personal, sometimes purely psychological—I began to see things differently.

Concepts I had never considered before suddenly became the foundation of my thoughts and actions. What is the mind? How do we handle fear, pain, or uncertainty? Why do we struggle with self-worth? These weren't just abstract questions anymore; they were the keys to unlocking the strength I didn't realize I had.

What made him extraordinary wasn't just his knowledge, but the way he shared it—with patience, clarity, and a genuine belief in my ability to apply it. He didn't hand me answers; he guided me toward finding them for myself. There were times I felt overwhelmed, questioning everything, but he had a way of breaking things down.

There were times I felt overwhelmed, questioning everything, but he had a way of breaking things down. I was lying on my bed, exhausted and in pain. The kind of day where every movement felt like too much. Yet, when my phone buzzed, and I saw his message, it brought a small spark of relief. I got a text from BM Sir.

Sir: *Heyy! How are you doing?* Me: Not good, Sir. I'm not able to sit, write, or watch anything. Sir: *Can you talk?* Me: Yes, Sir.

A few minutes later, we were on the call. Sir asked, *"Tell me, what's on your mind?"*

I sighed deeply, trying to find the words. "It's just one of those days, Sir. The pain is a lot, and my mind feels so restless. I don't know what to do."

He let a brief silence settle before responding. *"That's okay."*

Then he started the discussion with a question, *"What do you think is the goal of life?"*

The question caught me off guard. I paused, thinking about all the things we chase—success, stability, relationships.

Finally, I said, "To live a good life, maybe? To achieve something meaningful?"

He smiled, his tone calm but firm. *"That's part of it, but it's not the whole truth."*

I hesitated, unsure of what he meant. "Is it about making others happy?"

He said, *"Not quite. Let me ask you this—when you imagine the best version of your life, what's the one thing you want to feel?"*

I thought for a moment and said softly, "Happy, I suppose."

"Exactly. Everything we do—every goal, every dream, every relationship—is driven by one thing: the pursuit of happiness. But most people spend their lives looking for it in the wrong places." he then continued *"Tell me, where do you think happiness comes from?"*

"Achievements, maybe? Being with the right people? Feeling loved?" I said.

"*Those things can bring moments of joy, but they're not the source of happiness. Happiness comes from understanding your mind and aligning it with the truth of life. When you stop letting external circumstances control your emotions, you'll find that happiness is already within you. It's not about escaping pain, but finding peace in the midst of it.*" he said.

I frowned, trying to process his words. "But how can I feel happy when everything hurts, Sir? When even simple things feel impossible?"

He paused, then said gently, "*Happiness doesn't mean you'll never feel pain or sadness. It means accepting those feelings as part of life, not resisting them. On days like this, it's not about trying to 'fix' everything. It's about finding small moments of peace, even if it's just breathing and reminding yourself that this too shall pass.*

And remember this: if there's good, there's bad too. Life is a balance. If you allow yourself to feel happy, you also have to accept that some days won't feel as good. Both are part of the same journey."

I reflected on his words, and after a moment of silence, I asked him something that had been lingering in my mind for a while. "Sir, how do you maintain such a positive mindset, even when things get tough?"

He responded with a calm conviction, "*I believe that nothing comes alone—everything comes with its side effects. The side effect of pleasure is sorrow, of praise is insult, and of success is failure. Even marriage has its side effects; there's even a movie titled Shaadi Ke Side Effects.*

Being mentally prepared for these side effects helps me maintain a positive mindset during tough times. In most cases, people are not ready for these side effects, which is why they often give up easily in life."

His words stayed with me long after our call ended.

That night, I found myself reflecting on his question, turning it over in my mind. Was happiness really the goal? If it was, why did it often feel so elusive?

As I lay awake, I began to realize that happiness wasn't something external to be found—it was something to be nurtured within. And with that, I started understanding the ultimate goal of life.

Chapter 15
Ultimate goal

True happiness is an internal compass, not a distant destination.

Every human being thrives for happiness in his or her life. At the end of the day, whatever I'm doing is only and only for happiness and contentment. But the extent to which I had to go behind all these is to think of one fact: it didn't last long. After every dopamine rush, I needed another and went for it. There was no stop to that. Always running behind people's happiness and parents' happiness, but this period has taught me the real meaning of happiness.

The thing that we all long for is the same, but the meaning of how we get it is different.

Now the question is: how can we gain this simple solution?

In the evening, as my mom was cooking dinner, I couldn't keep my thoughts to myself any longer. I leaned against the kitchen counter and asked, "Mummy, how do you stay so calm? Don't you ever feel like happiness is slipping away?"

She paused, stirring the pot, then turned to me with a gentle smile and said, "*Happiness isn't something to hold onto. It's like water— it flows. You just have to dip your hands in when it passes.*" Her words lingered with me long after.

The problem was we were all looking for happiness and contentment in other people, things, relationships, and parents, but the answer was always in ourselves. You just have to go back to being a child. As simple as it sounds, but on the contrary, it is very difficult because, as the ultimate creations we are, humans are never taught to go backward in life. Everyone says growth should always be forward-moving, like a graph that rises steadily "Lives are marked by progress, not regression," which is not completely true. It steadily gives rise to expectations, sadness, and fear.

Now, think of a child who is just enjoying life without thinking of future goals. You would now remember your childhood, if you didn't try to recall how amazing, beautiful, and powerful a child you were.

The same has helped me today.

As a kid, there was no word like suppression. Now that I'm old enough to understand this, the suppressed feelings I've been carrying all these years have led to so much stress, fear, confusion, anger, and self-doubt—always feeling the need to seek validation when not necessary.

Children don't dream of being happy someday; they simply are. To achieve happiness, let go of tomorrow; live as a child does today.

I once tried to meditate to feel 'inner peace.' Instead, I ended up falling asleep. My sister teased me for days, saying I'd found peace in my dreams. It was funny, but it also made me realize something important: just sitting and meditating might help some people, but for me, true peace often comes from doing something I genuinely love. It's not always about sitting still and focusing on your breath; it can be about losing yourself in the joy of painting, playing guitar, cooking, or even laughing with loved ones. Inner peace doesn't have to follow a rulebook.

We often seek happiness in what lies ahead. True peace is sometimes found in the innocence of the past. Sometimes, to heal and find joy, you must let go of your adult burdens and return to the heart of a child, where joy is unspoken and unconditional.

But now another question arises in my mind: how? I can't just let go of all my burdens and worries.

Letting go of all negative emotions and worries doesn't happen overnight, but like I said, it starts by recognizing that not everything needs to be controlled. Worrying about what's out of our hands only adds to our stress and it won't even change the outcome.

But it was still very difficult to just surrender and let go, especially when I used to feel responsible for so many things. But I understood that it's important to remember it's not about immediately releasing everything at once.

It is a very gradual process and I had to be, and I'm still, very patient. We don't have to carry every worry or responsibility alone, and feeling that it is difficult is okay. No great feeling comes with ease; acknowledging is the first step.

In my journey, one thing I had to learn the hard way is that it's okay not to have everything figured out. The world never aligns with our plans, and life can throw curveballs we never expected.

And in this journey of acceptance, one of the most profound lessons I learned was to reconnect with the child within me.

As I grew older, I accumulated so many worries about my future, my career, and how others perceive me. The weight of these thoughts became overwhelming, but somewhere along the way, I realized the purity of a child's view on life was something I had long lost.

As a child, life was simple.

Happiness came effortlessly—from a sunny day, a favorite snack, or the sound of laughter during a game. There were no lists of goals, no fears of falling short, and certainly no overthinking. It was as if joy lived in the smallest, simplest moments. But as I grew older, the simplicity faded. Suddenly, happiness wasn't about the now—it became a puzzle of achievements, expectations, and constant comparisons.

I used to think this complexity was just part of growing up—that it was normal to carry the weight of plans, worries, and what-ifs. But during this journey, I started questioning that. Why did we trade the ease of a child's joy for the stress of an adult's chase? Was it really progress if it left us feeling emptier?

The answer wasn't about undoing responsibilities or avoiding the realities of adulthood. It was about reclaiming a child's mindset— a way of seeing life for what it is, instead of what we think it should be. Children don't overcomplicate; they simply exist. They don't analyze happiness or schedule it. They just feel it.

Imagine being that child again. What would it take for you to bring that simplicity into today?

So I began to experiment, trying to blend the wisdom of adulthood with the simplicity of childhood. It wasn't always easy. Letting go of the complexity meant challenging long-held beliefs and learning to focus on the present moment. But the more I tried, the clearer it became: happiness isn't hidden in some far-off future. It's right here, in the everyday.

Children live in the moment, not burdened by weight or having futile worries, expectations, or fear. They simply exist to play and experience life. Now, struggling with my own health and all that came with it, I started embracing that mindset. I gave myself permission to imagine approaching life with the wonder of a child. Instead of trying to find meaning and whys in everything, I learned to let go, and I remembered how a child can find joy in the smallest things: sunny days, colorful flowers, motorcycles, or a simple conversation. I allowed myself to feel that too.

And going back to being a child didn't mean avoiding responsibility or ignoring things in life; it meant letting go of the emotional weight that we all carry around everywhere. I found that, just like a child, I could face the hardest moments with a sense of curiosity and wonder. I didn't need to have everything figured out; I could simply experience life now as it comes.

That's when I realized how much this shift brought me.

As I began aligning my life with my ultimate goal—happiness—I had a sudden, eye-opening realization: no one achieves true happiness in isolation. Sure, the foundation of happiness starts within, but it's the connections we nurture that truly amplify it. I had spent so much time focusing on my personal growth, my mindset, and how I could tackle life's challenges on my own.

But as I navigated through the ups and downs of my journey, I discovered a deeper truth: happiness isn't just about conquering obstacles by yourself. It's also about having the right people by your side, those who lift you when you're falling and push you to be better, even when you don't see the potential in yourself.

It was through the relationships I built over time—especially my friendships—that I began to feel a new strength.

Chapter 16

Oh dearest in the battle so grand we will navigate the waves hand in hand

Many days passed, filled with writing, learning, and small moments of progress, yet worry always lingered in the background. But last night, the pain became constant—a new reminder of what chemo and cancer bring. Each day feels uncertain, a new surprise of pain, and the warrior is left wondering-what will come next?

But the pain was the same that I felt before my very first diagnosis so I was a little scared. What if?

But then I would push my worries aside and reach out to my friends. I'm lucky to have my people around—the ones I call my home. With them, I can talk about anything without hesitation. They are my safe space, the ones who listen when I share my worries, my pain, and my thoughts. They are the ones who stayed with me through it all. For that, I am endlessly grateful.

One such moment was with Ishika. I texted her, "Bello!" Almost instantly, she replied, "*Hiii! I was just thinking about you. How are you feeling?*"

I responded simply, "Good."

She quickly asked, "*Are you still having pain in the back?*"

I nodded, even though she couldn't see me, and typed back, "Yes." I could sense her worry through her words as she said, "*I love you. I'm sorry I can't do anything to help you. You are one hell of a warrior—you got this! Did you take the meds?*"

I replied, "Yes."

"*Life is being a big-time bitch to you, and you've been giving it back like no one has ever seen before. You're going to get through this like a real-life superhero.*

Your pain, your struggle, and the way you fight through it, very few in this world have. The resilience you have, I don't think anyone else possesses it. You are everyone's heart."

"*There's nothing in this world we wouldn't trade for you to feel better. You will fight and get out of this, and we all have immense faith in you. You are a miracle. You are going to resurrect like the phoenix that you are.*"

The conversation went on for a while, filled with her gentle concern and encouragement.

Ishika—how can I even begin to describe her? She lights up hope in the darkest corners of my life, reminding me that no matter how heavy the day feels, I'm not carrying it alone.

Whether it's a quick text or a long chat, she somehow always knows what to say. It's not just her words—it's her presence, her unwavering belief in me, and the love she radiates. she's a reminder that even in the middle of chaos, there's always hope

With Ishika, Kyra, and Adi, I always had my circle. We survived life together, finding comfort in dark humor, jokes that only we could laugh at, and meetups filled with both crying and laughing sessions.

One evening, when the weight of it all felt too much to bear, I texted Kyra. I wrote, "I'm feeling weak and on the verge of crying. More than crying, I don't know... It's all just too much. The back pain has started again, and I don't know how I'll manage the chemo this time. I know you can't do anything, but I needed to tell someone."

Her reply came quickly. "*You home?*"

"Yes," I responded, unsure of what she could say to make me feel better.

A moment later, her next message popped up: "*Open the door.*"

Confused, I slowly got up, walked to the door, and opened it. There she was, standing with a small bag of groceries in her hand, smiling at me as though she hadn't just dropped everything to come to my rescue.

"*I figured you might need this,*" she said, walking in like it was the most normal thing in the world.

Kyra didn't need to say much. She would bring me home-cooked meals, knowing I couldn't eat outside food much. Once, she brought pani puri from her home, a popular Indian street snack made of crispy, hollow shells filled with spicy water, tangy chutney, and mashed potatoes. It's the kind of food that instantly lifts your mood. We sat together, eating and laughing, and for a while, it felt like everything was normal. Moments like these reminded me how lucky I was to have her by my side.

While sitting at home, we called Adi and asked her to come over. She didn't take long to show up, juggling her work as we talked. We spent the evening together, sharing laughter, a few moments of quiet reflection, and even managed to click some photos.Later, we went to the terrace. It was late evening and the three of us sat there, staring at the sky.

I sighed, leaning back. "Four months ago, I was running after life. And now? Now I'm struggling to climb stupid stairs. How the hell did it all go so wrong so fast?"

Kyra gave a half-smile, nudging me. "Look, the stairs are overrated anyway. Nobody climbs them anymore. It's all elevators and escalators now."

Adi laughed. "Yeah, and honestly, bald is the look. You're saving so much by not having those impromptu hairdos! Think of the financial benefits."

I raised an eyebrow, the corner of my mouth twitching up. "Wow, great perspective, guys. Maybe I'll start my own influencer journey."

Kyra nodded dramatically, pretending to think. "Exactly! We'll shoot your first reel right here. 'How to rock when life decides to give you lemons—and steals your hair.'"

Adi jumped in, adding, "And don't forget the caption: 'Climbed 4 flights of stairs for this view. Zero regrets. Also, zero stamina."

I shook my head, laughing despite myself. "You two are ridiculous."

Kyra's tone softened, her eyes holding mine for a moment. *"We're ridiculous for you. And honestly? You're allowed to be mad at life right now. You're allowed to miss what you've lost. But don't ever forget—you're not missing us. We're right here. Always."*

Adi nodded, his voice steady. *"You've got us, okay? Through every step you climb, every chemo session, every shitty day. We're not going anywhere."*

I swallowed, feeling the lump in my throat. "I know. That's the only thing keeping me sane. You guys make this... bearable."

Kyra grinned. *"Bearable? Excuse me, we make it awesome. Admit it—you've never been this cool before."*

Adi shot me a playful look. *"Exactly! Cancer doesn't get to define you. We do. And we say you're badass. Bald and badass and stronger than the rest!"*

I shot them both with a look of mock annoyance. "God, I hate you both."

Kyra laughed, nudging me again. *"No, you love us. Now shut up and enjoy the view."*

We sat in comfortable silence after that, clicking some more pictures, the sound of laughter and life hanging in the air.

Adi posted those pictures along with something she had written for me.

Reading her words felt like a warm hug on a cold day. Here's what she wrote:

"Have the starkest of memories being on call almost a year ago, laughing at that breathlessness, laughing at you and your roomies coughing, waiting for the 'viral' to eventually shush off. Couple nights ago on call, my heart stopped while you cried, gasping for breath, trying to say you're not sure if you'll make it thru. I cannot imagine the number of days and nights you've had feeling so fkn tragic trying to deal w it on your own. I cannot imagine how hard you must be trying to stay strong, put on a happy face, be ok w all the shitty humour we pull on you. There's days you must be feeling what's the fucking point but I guess we'll have to be ok w never having an answer to it.

You've had to make some insanely hard decisions, deal w some insanely new things but know that not everybody has the balls for it and we're all SO proud of you.

There's probably nothing I can say to make you feel great but know that whatever you're feeling is valid so don't beat yourself up for that.

Yes, I know nice things are not something you'd expect me to say and I'll be more than happy if this cracks you up coming from me."

I couldn't help but smile reading her words. After all these years of dark humor and sarcasm, It took cancer to bring out Adi's soft side.

There were moments when the exhaustion threatened to swallow me whole, and I thought I couldn't go on. I texted Adi, telling her I was tired—too tired to keep pushing.

"I'm tired," I typed, feeling completely drained.

"Bud, please, please hold on," she replied almost immediately *"You can't let all the effort go to waste. You've got to pull your willpower together, however tough it may feel. I'm sorry, but I've never seen a soul stronger than you. Hope you know you can vent to me anytime."*

I didn't have the strength to respond. So I sent back the only thing I could, *"I know, but I have nothing to say."*

And then, in typical Adi fashion, she broke the silence with the words that always seemed to bring a little light: *"Well, you always say, love you, Adi."*

There's nothing in this world we wouldn't trade for you to feel better. You will fight and get out of this, and we all have immense faith in you. You are a miracle. You are going to resurrect like the phoenix that you are."

Ishika sent me a poem. One stanza in particular stayed with me:

"A vast horizon, your soul as big as the sky.
No matter what, we will always stand by.
Life's struggles may echo a relentless sound,
Yet within you, there's strength profound.
Oh dearest, in this journey we tread,
Your courageous lighthouse where shadows are led.
Battling with life- fighting the decrease

we have found a braveheart-a masterpiece "

True friendship isn't something that blooms only in the sunlight; it's tested and proven in the storms. It reveals itself when there's no applause, no reward—just the quiet, steadfast presence of those who choose to stand beside you, no matter how messy or broken life gets.

I learned that true friends are not the ones who fix your problems; they're the ones who make you feel less alone while you face them. Ishika's endless check-ins weren't just texts—they were lifelines reminding me that someone cared deeply. Kyra's home-cooked meals weren't just food—they were an extension of her love, offering me comfort when I couldn't find it anywhere else. Adi's heartfelt words didn't just make me smile—they gave me strength when I had none left.

But the greatest lesson my friends taught me was this: *empathy is the foundation of true friendship.* It's not about saying the perfect thing or always knowing what to do. It's about showing up—with open hearts, with listening ears, and with love that doesn't falter in the face of hardship.

It isn't a fair-weather bond—it's a promise to be there when the days are darkest. It's a reminder that the love we give and receive during life's hardest moments has the power to heal in ways no medicine can.

Through all of this I learned that empathy matters more than we realize. *In a world that often feels disconnected, be the person who stays. Be the friend who listens, who cares, who believes in someone when they forget to believe in themselves.* Because those acts of love and kindness don't just help others—they transform you, too.

Friends aren't just the ones who stand by you—they're the ones who elevate you, who push you to grow, and who remind you of the best version of yourself. They're the ones who don't let you settle for less, who celebrate your victories like they're their own, and who challenge you to dream bigger even when you're too scared to try.

When I look back, that's exactly what my friends did for me. Through their love, their words, and their unwavering faith in me, they helped me fight battles I didn't think I could win. They reminded me of my strength, even when I felt like giving up.

Friends don't just walk the journey with you—they make the road a little brighter, the hills a little easier to climb, and the destination worth reaching.

Choose friends who elevate your spirit and your life. And more importantly, be that kind of friend to others. Because when we lift each other up, we don't just grow individually—we rise together.

Chapter 17
Elephant in the room

The 21 days flew by in the blink of an eye, and soon, I was back on a train, heading toward another round of chemo. In the hospital bed, I distracted myself with my phone, exchanging texts with Jim like we always did.

But something felt different. Conversations that once felt effortless now carried an unspoken weight. We both knew we were standing at a crossroad. He was about to begin a new life abroad, while I remained here, fighting a battle that made everything uncertain.

As much as I wanted to hold on, I couldn't ignore the reality—we were drifting toward an inevitable goodbye. It wasn't about love or care; those things still existed. But sometimes, love isn't about holding on. Sometimes, it's about letting go before bitterness takes over.

Jim understood. He always did. And in his own way, he reassured me that we would always carry the good, even if our paths were no longer the same.

It hurt more than I expected. The finality of it. The realization that no matter how much we wanted to, we couldn't change what was coming. I couldn't understand why life had to be this way. Why couldn't things be different?

But In this moment, what stood out wasn't the pain or the sadness—it was the honesty between us. Neither of us was pretending, nor were we trying to sugarcoat what was happening. Jim he was someone who understood the reality of our situation, someone who cared enough to be truthful, even if it meant facing an uncomfortable truth. The love and respect we had for each other were undeniable, but sometimes love doesn't mean keeping things the same. Sometimes, it's about letting go with grace and understanding.

I realized the importance of clarity in relationships, especially during difficult times. We can't control the future, but we can choose how we handle the present. Jim's decision to acknowledge the inevitable wasn't an easy one, but it was the kind of honesty that real love demands. And even though it hurt, it was a kindness in disguise. We both knew that if we held on to something that was slipping away, it would only bring more pain. And so, we faced the truth together—without blame, without bitterness.

It wasn't about one person being right or wrong. It was about recognizing that, sometimes, the most caring thing you can do for someone is to set them free, even if it means letting go. We had our time, we shared our moments, and now, it was time for both of us to move forward. But what mattered was that we would always carry the good, the love, and the growth from what we'd shared.

Sometimes, letting go is the most difficult thing you can do, but also the most necessary. It's not about stopping loving or walking away in anger; it's about recognizing that both of you need different things now, and forcing the connection would only create more pain. The truth is, love doesn't always look like holding on tightly. Sometimes, it means giving each other the space to grow and change in ways that you can't keep up with anymore. It wasn't about giving up; it was about respecting that we both had our own paths to walk, even if they were no longer parallel.

With Jim, I found someone who had a level of maturity I admired—a person who not only laughed with me but also understood when words weren't enough. The bond we had wasn't defined by the relationship status or the distance between us; it was shaped by the respect, the care. Jim wasn't just the guy I wanted; he was the guy I needed at that moment, and for that, I'll always be thankful.

But twists in the story are always unexpected, just when you think you've experienced all that the day has to offer, time has a way of throwing something else your way. Later that evening, the doctors came in with Dad, and I couldn't comprehend anything. They weren't saying much, but the air in the room felt thick with tension. Their faces were serious, and I could sense something was off. It was a whirlwind of mixed feelings. I was too overwhelmed to process the situation fully.

The doctors performed the PET scans, hoping to gain a clearer understanding of the reasons behind the persistent back and shoulder pain. What was supposed to be a routine examination now carried the weight of uncertainty.

Then, as if the weight of the moment wasn't heavy enough, they addressed the elephant in the room:

"You've been diagnosed with bone metastasis."

Chapter 18

In the face of doubt, time becomes your most patient ally

As I tried to process the weight of their words, something caught my eye. The date. It was December 30th. Well, I thought bitterly, a very happy new year to me.

A tear slipped down my cheek as I glanced at my dad. Seeing him cry—his face, usually strong, was now etched with concern and helplessness. The room felt suffocating, the air heavy with unspoken thoughts. Everything the doctors were saying seemed distant, as though I were hearing it through a fog. I didn't know what to expect anymore. I didn't know how to face the unknown, how to navigate a future that had suddenly become so uncertain. All I knew was that in that moment, everything felt overwhelming.

I didn't know what lay ahead, and I didn't know how I would face it. But in that moment, I realized that as long as I held onto that quiet defiance, I could somehow find the strength to keep going, no matter how difficult it became.

That's when it hit me—the person who could help me through this situation was just a text away. I reached out to BM Sir, someone whose words had always given me the strength to move forward.

I quickly typed, "Hello, Sir. I haven't been able to stay in touch. I'm in the hospital."

His reply came almost instantly: "*Is everything alright?*"

I hesitated for a moment before replying, my fingers shaking as I shared the truth, "They did a PET scan yesterday. The doctors have stopped the chemo... Cancer has spread to my bones. They don't see radiation as an option. They're putting me on chemo tablets for two months. I don't know how I'm going to survive this, but I will."

His reply was simple yet reassuring: "*Yes, you will survive, no matter how.*"

But the question I couldn't shake off still gnawed at me. "But I don't understand. I've been trying to do everything right... Why is this happening? I know there's no answer to why, but I really need your help to make my mind strong enough to survive all this pain."

He replied calmly, as he always did, "*I'm always with you.*"

I wasn't convinced by just those words. The doubt still lingered in my mind. "The doctors have been looking at me like they're not really sure. Their faces, their words—they don't give me much hope."

He responded with something that resonated deep within me: "*That's their problem. Medical science has limitations, but the mind does not.*"

I paused for a moment, trying to grasp the weight of his words. "What should I do, Sir?" I asked.

"You've got the diary," he replied. *"Write down your imagination—where you want to see yourself. Keep your vision clear."*

I nodded even though I knew he couldn't see me. "And what else?"

"Focus on all the best and positive things in your life," he said. *"Write everything you are grateful for. List them in your diary. Keep yourself grounded in the good."*

I typed back, "Yes, Sir. I will."

I did as he said, I wrote things down.

The Day That Took a Turn in Life

I was hoping my pain would end soon. I was dealing with everything this year, but I got my PET scan result today, and my disease is showing progression.

I saw my dad coming to me and bursting into tears, and my mother also started crying. Clearly, the results were not so good. The day when I was hoping everything would end and I could start a new chapter of my life with recovery, but here I was sitting in the hospital, completely bedridden with bone metastasis. One whole year of chemotherapies to see this day. I was completely heartbroken, but I know I had to stay strong for my parents, just like they were for me. I know if I give up now, my year would go in vain. This whole year's constant hard work, hope, positivity, and whatnot would go in vain.

As I heard this from my dad, seeing him cry hopelessly, there was this strong energy in me. I don't know where it was coming from, but I felt like this is not the end. I'm going to get through this. I don't know how, but I'll get through this.

With these thoughts, as I went to sleep, there was sharp throbbing pain from my waist to legs. I couldn't sleep the whole night. The pain was so unbearable that I used to feel I could lose my life any moment now. I was literally begging my parents and doctors to ease my pain. They were trying their best, but no painkiller or medicine was giving me relief.

That's when I felt like someone had dragged and thrown me to the exact same place from where it all started, like from the cancer diagnosis at the very beginning, and there I was again. But this time, it wasn't like the last time. There was no anxiety, but there was this aggression in me.

I'm so stubborn that I'll get the life I want. There was such a determination inside me that said, "Don't just toss me once, toss me 10 times, I'll come back stronger than ever mentally." Though, when physically I was extremely low, I used to get extremely low thoughts, but I decided not to wrestle with it and feel the pain and emotions completely. The aim was to constantly keep trying and imagine the life that I want for myself.

As I sat in front of my screen, the warm glow of the setting sun filling the room as I spoke with Sir. He listened intently, as always, his calm demeanor a constant source of strength for me.

"Sir, I did what you said—I wrote everything down," I said, frustrated. "But the doubts... they're still there."

He smiled. "*Go ahead, ask your questions,*" he said, leaning back.

I hesitated for a moment, but then the floodgates opened. "What if all of this doesn't work out? What if I fail? What if I'm not strong enough? What if…"

He interrupted gently, "*Alright, alright… so many 'what ifs.' Tell me, do you know everything about tomorrow?*"

"No," I admitted reluctantly.

"*Exactly,*" he said. "*Doubts are like clouds—they come and go. Some will clear when you act, and others, well, they just need time. You see, not everything in life is meant to be resolved immediately. Sometimes, you need to live through it to see the answers unfold. But for now, tell me—what is within your control today?*"

I thought for a moment and replied, "My actions. My effort."

He nodded. "*And that's enough. The rest? Trust the process. Even the strongest storms eventually pass.*"

"But what if they don't?" I asked, my voice barely above a whisper.

He chuckled. "*Then you dance in the rain.*"

"But, sir," I was struggling to find words.

"*There are always multiple doubts,*" He said, "*but some can only be solved with time. You've heard it before—time heals the deepest wounds, and it's true.*"

I nod, though I can't help but feel a flicker of resistance. "But how, Sir? How does time solve anything? Isn't it just... passing by while we endure the pain?"

He smiles knowingly, sensing my resistance. "*Think of time not as something external, but as something within you. Time isn't just the ticking of a clock—it's a process, a flow, an intelligence that works silently. Every moment we live, time is shaping us, moving us closer to the resolution of our doubts. But here's the catch: time can only work its magic if we let it.*"

I tilt my head, intrigued but confused. "What do you mean by 'let it'?"

"*In life,*" he explains, "*most of us resist time. We fight against what is happening, constantly demanding answers, solutions, or results. But time isn't something you control—it's something you align with. When you stop resisting and start flowing with time, you allow it to do its work. You give it the space to reveal what needs to be revealed, to heal what needs to be healed.*"

Time doesn't wait for anyone, but it also never abandons anyone. It's always moving, always working, whether we notice or not.

I think about how often I've demanded certainty in my life, especially during my treatment. The fear, the anxiety, the endless questions—What's next? Will I survive? Will I ever feel whole again? These doubts haunted me day and night.

"*When you stop forcing and start trusting, time becomes your ally,*" Sir adds, his voice soft but steady. "*It teaches you what no one else can. It heals wounds you thought were permanent and shows you perspectives you never imagined. But it asks for your surrender, not in defeat, but in faith."*

I think of the silent intelligence of time. How it has carried me through moments I never thought I could survive—how even in the darkest nights, it nudged me forward, one breath at a time.

Time isn't separate from you—it's a part of you. When you surrender to it, you're not giving up.

I sit back, the weight of my doubts feeling just a little lighter.

Chapter 19

In the silence of pain, the whispers become our loudest voice.

A few days had passed since that conversation, and each day felt like an uphill battle. The doctors had warned me that the pain would be relentless for a while, so I had steeled myself to endure. They kept giving me painkillers, hoping they would take the edge off, but it never seemed to be enough. On top of that, my platelets had dropped, and they had to start giving me injections. Each new treatment made my body feel weaker, more fragile, as though it was losing its strength bit by bit.

It started with the tightness in my chest. At first, I told myself it was just another part of the process, another hurdle to cross. But deep down, a growing sense of unease kept gnawing at me, a feeling I couldn't shake no matter how much I tried to push it aside. Breathing became more difficult, like there wasn't enough air in the room to fill my lungs.

Sleep had become a stranger these past few nights, and now, even when I could manage to drift off, the exhaustion that followed felt more suffocating than restful.

One afternoon, the nurse came in, and for a moment, there was a flicker of relief. She decided to stop the injection for a while, and I let myself believe, just for a moment, that maybe things would get better. But I knew better than to get my hopes up too high—the battle wasn't over. It was never over.

I turned to Mummy, who had been a constant presence by my side, and told her that I needed to go to the washroom. Her hands, so steady and gentle, helped me move slowly, supporting me with a care that made my heart ache. She didn't speak much, just silently guiding me through the motions, her presence more comforting than words ever could be.

When I returned to the bed, I felt like my body had become too heavy for even the soft mattress to support. Lying down no longer felt right. It was as if the bed itself was sinking under the weight of my fatigue, pressing down on me in ways that made every movement feel like an effort.

I asked Mom if I could sit in the chair instead, just for a while, needing a change of position, something to make this unbearable weight feel lighter.

I settled into the chair, trying to find some comfort, but it didn't come. My body still felt like it was made of lead, every part of me aching, every breath a struggle. The room was too quiet, the stillness almost too much to bear. I could feel the tightness in my chest returning, more intense now, like something inside of me was closing in. It was no longer a minor discomfort—it was fear, raw and undeniable, creeping through me.

As I sat there, trying to settle into the chair, I felt the shortness of breath creeping back, but this time, it wasn't just a minor discomfort. It was different, more intense. It felt like my chest was tightening, like I wasn't getting enough air, like the weight of the world was suddenly on my lungs. I tried to breathe slowly, but it was too difficult. My vision started to blur, and my ears grew hot, like I could hear the blood rushing through them. Panic started to set in, and I could feel the fear rising in my chest, too. I could barely keep my thoughts together as I looked at Bhumi and Mummy. They saw it, too—saw the panic in my eyes—and rushed to call Papa.

I could hear the urgency in their voices as they asked him to come, and I tried to hold on, to fight it, but the pressure in my chest only grew stronger. Time seemed to stretch in that moment, each second feeling heavier than the last. Papa arrived quickly. But even with him by my side, I couldn't shake the fear that this might be it. I couldn't breathe. I could hardly keep my eyes open. The room felt like it was spinning, and I was trying to keep control of my thoughts, trying to stay grounded, but everything was slipping away.

Mummy stayed right next to me, her hands on mine, her voice soft as she prayed quietly under her breath. It was like she was trying to calm the storm in my chest, but nothing seemed to help. My body felt so weak, and every breath felt like I was fighting against something I couldn't see, couldn't understand. The nurse came back in with the oxygen mask, but even then, the relief was only temporary. The oxygen helped, but I still couldn't shake the overwhelming sense of panic.

And then the doctors came in. They gave me an injection to help me breathe easier, and slowly, little by little, I started to feel some relief. My chest loosened up, and I could breathe again, though it was still a little labored. The pressure wasn't as intense as before, but I could still feel the remnants of it hanging in the air. Dad asked the doctors what had caused this sudden shift, his voice steady but laced with concern. The doctors explained that it was a reaction to the injections they had given me earlier, which had caused my blood pressure to drop suddenly.

They assured us that we were quick to respond and that nothing was seriously wrong, but the panic still lingered in the room. I felt so small in that moment—vulnerable, unsure, and scared. But as the minutes passed and I started to breathe normally again, the fear slowly began to fade, and I felt myself sink into the bed, exhausted but relieved.

Later that night, I woke up to drink some water and checked my phone. There was a text from Bhumi. She had sent it around 3:29 AM.

"Didi, you know I love you a lot. You are a miracle magnet. Everything will get better soon."

I read it, and my heart swelled. I replied quickly, telling her not to worry about me, not to be scared. I told her that nothing was going to happen to me, that this was just a phase, a rough moment that would pass. I wanted to ease her mind, to make her believe that everything would be okay, even though I knew deep down that today's incident had scared me too.

"Love you. Don't worry about me. Nothing's going to happen. You have to stay strong for me. You have to take care of me if something like this happens again. It's just a phase, and it will pass soon."

I hit send and then set the phone down beside me. But the fear still clung to me, and I couldn't shake the feeling that something was slipping away from me.

I turned to Dad, who was still awake, and said, "Dad, I have a question…"

"Papa, what if this phase never ends?" I asked softly, my voice trembling as I lay on the bed. The room was dim, and my tired eyes searched his face for reassurance.

Dad sighed, the weight of my question settling on his shoulders. He pulled a chair closer to my bedside and sat down. For a moment, he just looked at me, his face calm but filled with a tenderness that only a father could have. Mummy, sitting at the edge of the bed, reached out and gently touched my arm.

"Beta," he began gently, *"then you will transform into something very strong and beautiful just as you are right now. You're scared, and that's okay. But let me tell you something—this phase, like all others, will pass. Life is like that. Phases come and go, but you, the real you, are beyond all of this. Let me explain it in a way you'll understand."*

I nodded, my curiosity slowly replacing the fear.

"Before you were born," he continued, *"where were you?"*

My brow furrowed. "I don't know," I said.

"Exactly," he said with a faint smile. *"But you were somewhere, right? Just because we didn't see you doesn't mean you didn't exist. And then, one day, you came into this world—you became visible to us. But your existence didn't start the moment we could see you; it started long before that."*

I listened intently, my breathing steady now.

"This body," he said, gesturing gently toward me, *"is like a temporary house. It lets you be visible for a while—80, 90, maybe 100 years if we're lucky. But after that, something changes. The body stops working, and we stop seeing the person. People think that means the person is gone, but no, beta, they're still there. Just invisible again. Just like before you were born."*

I tilted my head slightly, absorbing his words, and I felt Mummy squeeze my hand.

"Do you know what that means?" he asked.

"What?" I whispered.

"It means death is not an end," he said softly. *"It's just a change—a return to being unseen. The soul, the real you, is eternal. That's why they say death is an illusion. It feels real because we get attached to the things we see—the body, the face, the smile—but those are just temporary. The connection we feel, the love we have, is what's real. That doesn't die, even when the body does."*

I stared at him, my eyes glistening. "So... nothing is ever truly lost?"

He nodded. *"Nothing, beta. Not you, not me, not anyone. It's all still there, even when we can't see it. Like a ship sailing beyond the horizon. It doesn't disappear; it's just out of sight."*

I squeezed his hand, a sense of peace washing over me, but still, there was a lingering question. "*But what about the people we lose? Will they know we miss them?*"

Mummy, whose eyes were filled with understanding, leaned in slightly, her voice soft yet comforting. *"Oh, beta, they know. Love is timeless. It doesn't end when someone is no longer in front of us. Our hearts are connected in ways that we can't always understand. Those we love—those who are no longer visible—they live on in the love they gave us. And in the love we still carry for them. That never fades."*

Tears welled up in my eyes, but this time they were not of fear, but of understanding. "So we're never really apart?"

"*Never,*" Dad said with certainty, while Mummy nodded gently, her hand still holding mine. "*Not truly. And as long as you remember that, as long as you hold onto love, you will always be whole. You are more than just this moment, more than the things you can see. You are part of something much bigger, something that goes beyond time and space. And that, my dear, will never change…*"

A quiet calm filled the room as Dad's words sank in. I closed my eyes for a moment, letting them settle deep inside me. When I opened them again, there was a sense of peace that I hadn't felt before. I realized, in that moment, how incredibly grateful I felt.

Grateful for my parents, who gave me the strength I needed, not just in my body, but in my soul.

The fear that had been gnawing at me was still there, but it was no longer as overwhelming. It felt smaller, like I could finally breathe again. It was as if I had found an inner strength that I hadn't known existed within me.

And then I whispered, almost to myself, the words that felt true, deep down to the core of who I was, as if they had always been inside me, waiting to be spoken. I smiled and finally said, "I'm going to get better, don't worry Papa. You are my courage, and Mummy is my strength."

Dad smiled softly, his eyes filled with both love and determination. Mummy, too, smiled, her expression a perfect blend of warmth and hope. *"Yes, beta, we will come back, stronger than ever."*

Chapter 20
Living beyond the limits

After the first six cycles of chemotherapy, I believed the worst was behind me. I thought the maintenance chemotherapy would be less grueling, but how wrong I was. When the doctors broke the news of twelve more rounds of chemotherapy with no clear end in sight, a feeling of dread settled in me. How would I survive this?

But somewhere deep within, I found something I hadn't expected: the will to trust time. I learned to lean into hope, to hold onto the belief that there was something more beyond this. I realized that my mind could heal me as much as my body could. As I entered my sixteenth chemotherapy cycle, something in me shifted. I began to work on my imagination, reading, listening to stories of others who had been through similar battles, and learning from them. These stories didn't just inspire me, they became my strength.

I noticed the small changes in myself: the ability to rise after each treatment, to continue pushing towards the things I loved. It became a rhythm—a battle of resilience that started anew every 21 days. The cycle was grueling. I would hit rock bottom, feeling the devastating side effects of chemotherapy for eight-to-nine days. Then, on the tenth day, I would stand up and begin again, working towards being the strongest version of myself, ready to face whatever came next.

However, just when I thought things were beginning to settle, unexpected news arrived that shook me to the core. The doctors came to me with a new diagnosis:bone metastasis. It was a hard blow, a reality that I had not anticipated. The cancer had spread to my bones, complicating everything further. Suddenly, the treatment didn't seem like enough, and the uncertainty loomed larger. My mind spiraled, and the feeling of helplessness returned.

In moments of despair, I often found myself asking the question that so many people do: *Why is God—or the universe, or whatever exists—making me suffer so much?*

And then it dawned on me: God or the universe does not make us suffer. It is an illusion that a supreme power is sitting somewhere, keeping track of all our actions. It wasn't a punishment or a test that life had designed specifically for me. In reality, there are natural laws that operate automatically and are applicable to everyone. Understanding these laws and aligning our lives accordingly brings us joy. Conversely, whether by design or by default, when we break these laws, we suffer.

For example, if you, I, or anyone else puts their hand on fire, it will burn. It will never happen that a righteous person survives unharmed after surrendering themselves to fire, while a bad person perishes. The body has its own limitations, which apply to everyone—be it the rich, the poor, or even those we regard as God. Even Buddha, Mahavira, and Ramakrishna Paramhansa all succumbed to certain diseases. This understanding brought me a strange kind of clarity. When I realized this, I understood that my suffering wasn't because the universe was "against me" or that I was being singled out. It wasn't personal—it was simply the result of the way the world works. We all experience limitations in life because we live in bodies that are vulnerable to disease, aging, and injury. It doesn't matter how good or bad we are as people; the body we live in has its own set of rules, and those rules affect us all, regardless of our external circumstances or internal state.

This realization helped me release the feelings of guilt, anger, or confusion that had been associated with my diagnosis. It took me out of the mindset of asking, *Why me?* and placed me into a more accepting, practical framework. The question shifted from "Why is this happening to me?" to "How can I navigate this?" Instead of feeling targeted or singled out by life's challenges, I began to see that suffering is part of the shared human experience. We are all vulnerable to life's unpredictable nature, and suffering is something that connects us, not isolates us.

Understanding that suffering isn't a personal punishment or cosmic injustice but rather a natural part of the human condition made it easier to face the hardships that lay ahead. I could accept the reality of my situation more fully and focus on finding ways to manage it rather than resisting it or blaming myself for it. I knew that if I embraced the reality of life's natural laws, I could learn to live with it and even thrive despite it.

But even in new challenges, I chose not to surrender to fear. I decided that I couldn't keep waiting for the "right time" to live, to heal, or to move forward. Time, I realized, was not something to wait for—it was something to make the most of. If I was going to be at home for an indefinite period, waiting through treatments and recovery, I had to create something with that time. I couldn't let it slip by.

That's when I began writing. It became my release, my outlet. Writing, along with everything I had been learning—about life, health, relationships, and self-acceptance—started to shape the next phase of my journey. I stopped seeing my life as a series of treatments to endure. Instead, I saw it as a path to walk, one day at a time, with intention, resilience, and hope.

I could not predict the future, nor did I know when my treatment would end, but I did know this: my story wasn't over. I wasn't going to wait for some magical moment or the "perfect time" to make my life meaningful. I was going to live through the hard days, through the struggles and uncertainty, and find meaning in the midst of it all.

And here I was, writing the end of the first part of my story in my journal. It wasn't the end of my life—it was the beginning of my transformation.

The first part of my story was about survival. The next part would be about thriving.

Dear diary,

This is my journey so far. I am still in the midst of my treatment; it is a long way after the treatment as well, but I have learned so much up to this point and will continue to do so. One of the most important things cancer has taught me is that you don't have to be a certain way to enjoy your life and be happy and content. Happiness and peace should not be conditional.

Life has this incredible way of teaching us through experiences, through moments that shape us, challenge us, and sometimes even break us—only to rebuild us into something stronger and wiser. I've come to understand that there are three distinct paths to personal growth and redemption. These paths are not mutually exclusive; they intertwine and overlap, and the beauty lies in embracing all of them as they come into your life.

*The first is **karma yoga**, the path of action. Every action we take, every decision we make, becomes a lesson in itself. Through experience, we learn what aligns with our true self and what doesn't. I've made mistakes, stumbled, and fallen, but every time, life gently—or sometimes harshly—reminded me of what truly matters. Learning everything from our own actions or karma is not sufficient as life is limited, yet every moment teaches us, and every lesson leaves an imprint.*

*The second path is **bhakti yoga,** the path of devotion. This one is the hardest, requiring blind faith and trust in something larger than yourself. It's about letting go of control and embracing the flow of life, believing that whatever happens, happens for a reason. Surrendering doesn't mean giving up; it means accepting everything that happens to us whether positive or negative. It* *means complete absence of tension, frustration, worry or any negative emotion we feel. It means a permanent state of happiness, peace and joy. When the waves of uncertainty and fear crash over me, I remind myself that there is strength in allowing the tide to carry me rather than resisting it.*

The third path is **gyana yoga**, *the path of knowledge and wisdom. Knowledge has this fascinating ability to illuminate the dark corners of our mind. It's not about instant transformation but about planting seeds of understanding that grow with time. Knowledge is available in abundance in the universe that can save our time and energy and help us to live a life of happiness and peace. From Krishna to Buddha, Mahavira to Christ, and many have illuminated our lives through their unlimited wisdom. Wisdom allows us to navigate life's complexities with a little more clarity, even when it's not easy to fully digest or implement. It's about stepping back, observing, and realizing that every experience, every struggle, and every triumph is part of a much larger picture. I have found gyana yoga (transforming our lives through true knowledge) much easier to enlighten our lives because we do not have unlimited time on this earth to learn everything from our own actions. This can lead us finally to the hardest one, bhakti yoga which is surrendering everything to God no matter what happens to us.*

We are so often taught to set goals, to achieve, to conquer. But rarely are we told to pause, reflect, and accept that not everything will go as planned. Life is not one-sided. Every choice, every action, has its side effects. Sometimes we're prepared; sometimes we're not. And that's okay.

Cancer taught me this better than anything else ever could. There's no rushing the process, no shortcut to acceptance, no escaping the side effects of living. The key is to find peace in the chaos, to allow yourself to fall and then rise again, to embrace the imperfections of life as part of its beauty.

Ultimately, life's greatest lesson is this: your experiences are your true teacher. Trust the process, even when it's messy and painful. Learn to walk independently, yet never hesitate to lean on others when needed. Life isn't a straight line; it's a winding path full of surprises, and the only certainty is that it's worth walking.

As I write this, I feel a profound sense of calm. Maybe it's the realization that I don't need to have it all figured out right now. Maybe it's the quiet confidence that, no matter what happens, I'll keep walking this path with hope in my heart. And maybe, just maybe, years from now, when I look back, I'll smile and say, "I lived."

Today, I am happy and content with whoever I am, and I accept it. I have my fingers crossed in the hope that years later, when I reread this journal, I'll be proud of myself for not giving up, no matter what toss.

To be continued ...?

www.ingramcontent.com/pod-product-compliance
Lightning Source LLC
LaVergne TN
LVHW061550070526
838199LV00077B/6978